Green Line
Transition

Klausurvorschläge

von
Matthias Bode
Paul Dennis
Ralf Kerstgens
Hartmut Klose
Florian Otte
Michael Rybicki
Reiner Verspai

Ernst Klett Verlag
Stuttgart · Leipzig

Liebe Lehrerinnen und Lehrer,

der Titel *Green Line Transition* **Klausurvorschläge** mit CD-ROM bietet Ihnen zu den sechs *Topics* des Schülerbuchs editierbare Klausurvorschläge zu den kommunikativen Kompetenzen *Reading*, *Writing*, *Listening*, *Speaking* und *Mediation*.

Das Heft ist modular aufgebaut, d. h. zu jeder kommunikativen Kompetenz liegt ein ausgearbeiteter Aufgabenvorschlag vor. Somit können Sie für Ihren Test immer genau die Kompetenzen auswählen, die Sie zu prüfen wünschen.

Jedes *Topic* bietet Ihnen zwei Lesetexte an: einen Sachtext sowie einen literarischen Text. Das Leseverstehen zu den Texten lässt sich immer anhand einer „klassischen" *Comprehension*-Aufgabe oder eines geschlossenen/halboffenen Aufgabenformats überprüfen.

Ebenso finden Sie zu jedem *Topic* zwei unterschiedliche Hörtexte mit geschlossenen oder halboffenen Aufgaben vor.

Wie Sie sicher feststellen werden, lassen sich viele Materialien auch *Topic*-übergreifend einsetzen. So lässt sich beispielsweise die Kurzgeschichte „21" in *Free choice?* auch gut mit dem Thema *The digital age* verknüpfen.

Im Anhang und auf der CD-ROM finden Sie Bewertungsraster zu verschiedenen Kompetenzen. Diese können Sie entsprechend Ihres Erwartungshorizonts ergänzen und/oder als Hilfe für Ihre Korrektur verwenden.

Auf der dem Heft beiliegenden **CD-ROM** finden Sie:
- alle Klausurvorschläge und *Speaking cards* in editierbarer Form
- die Hörtexte und Transkripte
- die Bewertungsraster
- und die Lösungsvorschläge.

Wir wünschen Ihnen und Ihren Schülerinnen und Schülern viel Erfolg auf dem Weg in die Oberstufe!

Ihr *Green Line Transition*-Team

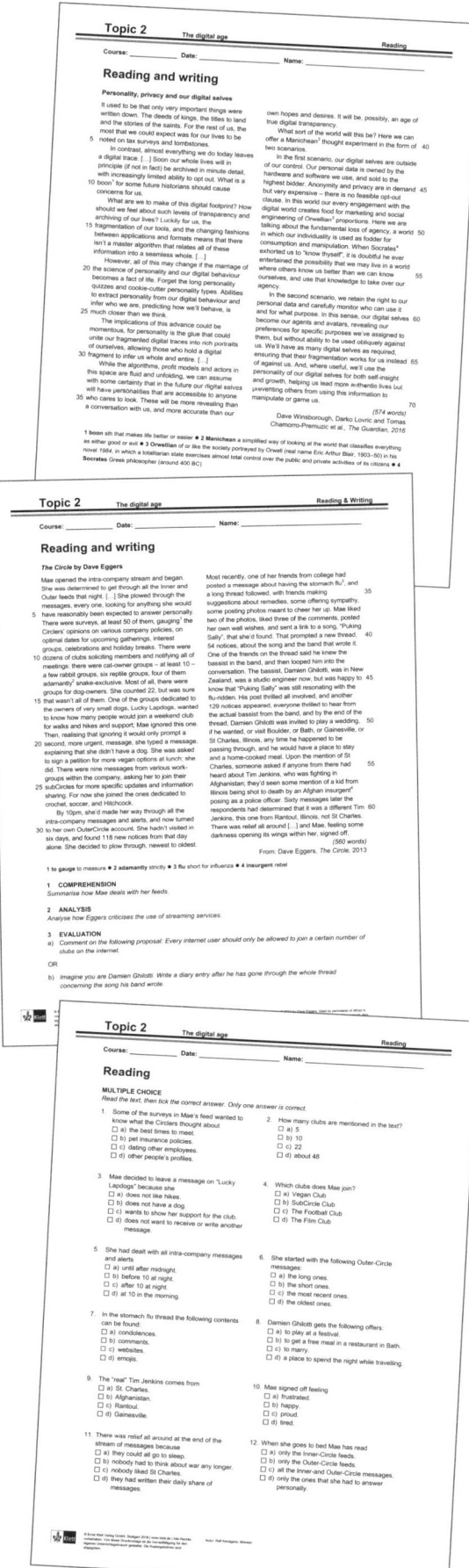

1 Free choice?

2 The digital age

3 Bridging the gap

4 Think globally, act locally

Zeichenerklärung:

⊙ Verweis auf CD-ROM (Audio)
  Einzelarbeit
  Partnerarbeit
  Gruppenarbeit

Abkürzungen:

AE American English
BE British English
sb somebody
sth something
i.e. id est (Lat.) = that is
e.g. exempli gratia (Lat.) = for example

Bildquellen Speaking Cards:
Test 1.1 shutterstock (M-SUR), New York, NY; **Test 1.2** shutterstock (Frannyanne), New York, NY; **Test 1.3** shutterstock (RTimages), New York, NY; **Test 1.4** ShutterStock.com RF (Barnaby Chambers), New York, NY; **Test 1.5** shutterstock (Rawpixel.com), New York, NY; **Test 1.6** ShutterStock.com RF (Natali Snailcat), New York, NY; **Test 1.7** shutterstock (Gods_Kings), New York, NY; **Test 1.8** shutterstock (Lightspring), New York, NY; **Test 2.1** ShutterStock.com RF (Tanja Esser), New York, NY; **Test 2.2** ShutterStock.com RF (BlueRingMedia), New York, NY; **Test 3.1** shutterstock (Paul Prescott), New York, NY; **Test 3.2** Alamy stock photo (WENN Ltd), Abingdon, Oxon; **Test 4.1** shutterstock (hafakot), New York, NY; **Test 4.2** shutterstock (Lucky Business), New York, NY; **Test 4.3** shutterstock (Gustavo Frazao), New York, NY; **Test 4.4** shutterstock (Dmitry Chulov), New York, NY; **Test 5.1** shutterstock (Gustavo Frazao), New York, NY; **Test 5.2** shutterstock (elwynn), New York, NY; **Test 6.1** shutterstock (Twinsterphoto), New York, NY; **Test 6.2** shutterstock (kitzcorner), New York, NY; **Test 7.1** ShutterStock.com RF (vector_sign), New York, NY; **Test 7.2** Alamy stock photo (Eric Nathan), Abingdon, Oxon; **Test 8.1** Alamy stock photo (Charles O. Cecil), Abingdon, Oxon; **Test 8.2** shutterstock (Monkey Business Images), New York, NY

Sollte es in einem Einzelfall nicht gelungen sein, den korrekten Rechteinhaber ausfindig zu machen, so werden berechtigte Ansprüche selbstverständlich im Rahmen der üblichen Regelungen abgegolten.

Course: _____ Date: _____ Name: _____

Reading and writing

Why Teens Find The End Of The World So Appealing

The plots of dystopian[1] novels can be amazing. A group of teens in Holland, Mich., tells me about some of their favorites:

In *Delirium* by Lauren Oliver, love is considered a
5 disease. Characters get a vaccine for it. In Marissa Meyer's *Renegade*[2], the collapse of society has left only a small group of humans with extraordinary abilities. They work to establish justice and peace in their new world.

10 Scott Westerfeld's *Uglies* is on everyone's favorite list. The plot goes like this: Everyone wants to be pretty. And their 16th birthday, they can be surgically altered to be a "pretty." During the surgery, however, lesions[3] are put on their brains. These can
15 cause illness, or hinder your thinking. If characters get an important enough job later on, they get those lesions removed.

The teens explaining these books are sitting around a table at the public library in the idyllic west
20 Michigan town. Tonight the book club is meeting to talk about *House of the Scorpion* by Nancy Farmer. […]

After a brief plot description (there's a drug lord, clones and, of course, a rebellion against the status
25 quo), Taylor Gort, 17, starts things off: "It's a question of how many ethics rules are you willing to break," she says, referring to the book's main character, El Patrón. Amanda Heidema, the librarian leading the discussion, nods her head, "I mean, is making a clone
30 ethical?"

There are a few beats of silence before Will Anderson shakes his head: "No, I don't think it is." The conversation goes on for nearly an hour — flowing from clones, to whether or not manipulation is
35 evil, to how screwed up adults are (can you believe they think this book is dystopian? It's not.).

That last one —how messed up grownups are — it's a hallmark[4] of dystopia, especially in the young adult genre. When I ask the group why they think
40 these types of books are so popular with teens, they tell me it has a lot to do with relatability[5].

"There tends to be a common teen-angst thing, like: 'Oh the whole world is against me, the whole world is so screwed up,'" Will explains.
45 Teenagers are cynical, adds Aaron Yost, 16. And they should be: "To be fair, they were born into a world that their parents kind of really messed up." Everyone here agrees: The plots in dystopia feel super familiar. That's kind of what makes the books scary — and really good. 50

Think of it like this: Teen readers themselves are characters in a strange land. Rules don't make sense. School doesn't always make sense. And they don't have a ton of power.

"Their parents impose curfews, and no one lets 55 them drive unless they are ready or not," says Jon Ostenson, who studies young adult dystopian literature at Brigham Young University in Utah. He published a paper on the subject in 2013, for which he spent months reading YA dystopia. "I had to take a 60 break for quite a while — unfortunately there's not a lot of utopian fiction to balance that out."

In dystopia, he says, "Teenagers see echoes of a world that they know."

These books don't always have a happy ending, 65 and they're all about choices and consequences.

"The hallmark of moving from childhood to adulthood is that you start to recognize that things aren't black and white," says Ostenson "and there's a whole bunch of ethical grey area out there." 70

Which makes dystopian fiction perfect for the developing adolescent brain, says Laurence Steinberg, a psychologist at Temple University. "Their brains are very responsive to emotionally arousing stimuli," he explains. […] 75

"When teenagers feel sad, what they often do is put themselves in situations where they feel even sadder," Steinberg says. They listen to sad music — think emo! — they watch melodramatic TV shows. So dystopian novels fit right in, they have all that 80 sadness plus big, emotional ideas: justice, fairness, loyalty and mortality.

This time in a kid's life is often defined by acting out, but, Steinberg says, that's a misguided interpretation of what's happening. "It isn't so much 85 rebellion, but it is questioning. […]

The fact that these books offer a safety net, a place where kids can "flirt with those questions without getting into trouble," that's reason enough to keep teachers and parents buying them off the shelf. 90

(732 words)
Elissa Nadworny, *NPR*, 2017

---

1 dystopian relating to a terrible or dreadful future ● **2 renegade** rebel ● **3 lesion** cut, injury ● **4 hallmark** proof of quality, indication ● **5 relatability** the ability to identify with or understand sth

Autor: Michael Rybicki, Buchholz in der Nordheide
Textquelle: ©2017 National Public Radio, Inc. Excerpts from NPR news report "Why Teens Find The End Of The World So Appealing" by Elissa Nadworny were originally published on npr.org on December 18, 2017, and is used with the permission of NPR. Any unauthorized duplication is strictly prohibited.

Course: _____ Date: _____ Name: _____

1   COMPREHENSION

Outline the main ideas of the novels mentioned in lines 1–22 and state why teens approve of them.
Write a coherent text of about 150 words using your own words as much as possible.

2   ANALYSIS

Referring to lines 45–90, explain why "the plots in dystopia feel super familiar" (ll. 48–49) to teenagers.
Write a coherent text of about 150 words using your own words as much as possible.

3   EVALUATION

Aaron Yost, 16, describes the situation of teenagers: "To be fair, they were born into a world that their parents
kind of really messed up." (ll. 46–47)
In a letter to the editor discuss if this is true in your view and if young people really need dystopian works of art
(short stories, novels, films) to understand their place in the world.

Reading

TRUE OR FALSE?

Read the text and decide whether the statements in the table are true or false. Give the line numbers and
the first and last three words of the quote to support your choice. There is one example (0).

		TRUE	FALSE
0.	The young adults interviewed by Elissa Nadworny come from the state of Holland. l./ll.: _1-3 "A group of teens … of their favourites."_		✓
1.	To cure love, people are hypnotised. l./ll.: _____		
2.	Rebels try to restore law and order. l./ll.: _____		
3.	Amanda Heidema is upset about El Patrón's moral standards. l./ll.: _____		
4.	Works of dystopian literature written for teenagers deal with adults who are morally deficient. l./ll.: _____		
5.	Teenagers have a great amount of influence on society at a rather early age. l./ll.: _____		
6.	Reading young adult utopian fiction is a significant part of Jon Ostenson's work. l./ll.: _____		
7.	Having read about choices and consequences, teenagers are often confused about responding to difficult moral questions. l./ll.: _____		
8.	Dystopian novels convey the same unhappiness that teenagers often feel. l./ll.: _____		
9.	Disobedient behaviour is not primarily what teenagers have in mind. l./ll.: _____		

Course: _____ Date: _____ Name: _____

Reading and writing

21 by Jim Crace

A youngish man, a trifle[1] overweight, too anxious for his age, completed his circuit of the supermarket shelves and cabinets and stood in line, ashamed as usual.

5 He arranged his purchases on the checkout belt and waited, with his eyes fixed on the street beyond the shop window, while the woman at the till[2] scanned all the bar codes on his medicines, his vitamins, his air freshener, his toilet tissue, his frozen
10 Meals for One, his tins, his magazines, his beer, and his deodorant, his bread, bananas, milk, his fat-free yogurt, his jar of decaf[3], and his treats: today, some roasted chicken legs, some grapes, a block of chocolate, and two croissants. He rubbed his thumb
15 along the embossed[4] numbers of his credit card while each item triggered a trill[5] of recognition from the till.

The till's computer recognized the young man's Distinctive Shopping Fingerprint as well, the usual ratio of fat to starch, the familiar selection of canned
20 food, the recent and increasing range of health supplements, the unique combination of monthly magazines. The pattern of the shopping identified the customer. Even before the woman at the till had swiped[6] the credit card, the computer had lined up
25 the young man's details – his list of purchases for the previous seven months, his credit rating, his Customer Loyalty score. It knew broadly who he was and how he lived. It could deduce what his modest rooms above the travel shop were like, how stale they
30 were, how flowerless, how functional, how crying out for change. Here was the man whose cat had died or

run away three months ago. No cat food purchased since that time. Here was the customer who had not left the neighborhood for more than seven days in living, byte-sized memory. Last spring, he'd tried – 35
and failed – to cut down on patisseries[7] and sugar. Today, for once, he had resisted his usual impulse purchase of a packet of cheroots[8].

Computer screened a message on the woman's till: Cheroots … Cheroots … it said. Remind the 40
customer he has not purchased cereals or cheese or vegetables this month. Remind him of our special offers: 12 cans of lager for the price of 10. Buy one bottle of our Boulevard liqueur and get a second free. Remind him that time is passing more quickly than he 45
thinks – his washing powder should be used by now, as should the contraceptives that he bought two years ago. He must need basics, such as rice and pasta, soap, toothpaste, flour, oil, and condiments[9]. Inform him of our Retail Schemes[10] and that we open 50
now on Sunday afternoons. Advise him that he ought to do more cooking for himself. He ought to tidy up and clean the bathroom tiles with our new lemon whitener. He ought to start afresh. Suggest to him he tour our shelves again. At once. For what we choose 55
is what we are. He should not miss this second opportunity to re-create himself with food.

(498 words)

Jim Crace, in: *Flash Fiction Forward: 80 Very Short Stories by James Thomas (Editor), Robert Shapard (Editor)*, 2006

---

1 trifle just a little ● **2 till** cash register ● **3 decaf** coffee (or tea) that has all or most of its caffeine removed ● **4 embossed** printed (so that it is raised above the surface) ● **5 trill** *trillern* ● **6 swiped** pulled through ● **7 patisseries** fancy cookies or pies, rich in sugar ● **8 cheroot** a cigar with both ends cut square; ● **9 condiments** a seasoning or relish for food such as pepper, mustard, sauces ● **10 retail schemes** special offers

1 COMPREHENSION
State in your own words what the "youngish man" (l. 1) has already done and what he is still expected to do. Write approximately 150 words.

2 ANALYSIS
Examine how the author characterises the "youngish man" (l. 1). Write a coherent text using your own words as much as possible.

3 EVALUATION
"For what we choose is what we are." (ll. 55–56) Comment on this statement taking your own shopping habits into account.

Course: _____   **Date:** _____   **Name:** _____

Reading

SHORT ANSWERS

Read the text and then answer the questions in 1–6 words. You need not write whole sentences.

1. Where is the man in the beginning of the story? _the man stood in line of the check cash register_

2. What does the lady at the till do? _she scanned all the things he had bought._

3. Which fruits does the man put on the belt? _bananas_

4. How does the man intend to pay for his purchase? _with his credit card_

5. How does the computer recognize the man? _each item trigged a trill of recognition from the till._

6. For how many months has the computer been storing the man's personal data? _for seven months_

7. According to the computer, how long has the man not been away from home? _The customer hadn't been left his neighborhood for more than seven days in living._

8. What has the man forgotten to buy in the last four weeks? Name two products. _cereals or cheese or vegetables_

9. Which alcoholic beverages should he also add to his favourites? _Boulevard liquer_

10. How many days a week does the store offer its services? _6 days a week (Monday Tuesday Wednesday, Thursday, Friday and Sunday)_

11. How should the man make his restroom spotless? _____

Course: _____ Date: _____ Name: _____

Listening

⊙ **What's up for dinner?**

MULTIPLE CHOICE
Listen to the interview and tick the correct answer. There is one example (0.) at the beginning.

0. 80% of all people in Washington do not know what's for dinner. Radio show host Audie Cornish has learned this from
   - ☑ a) the food data company Food Genius.
   - ☐ b) a collaboration with Youth Radio.
   - ☐ c) NPR reporter Sonari Glinton.

1. The speaker is reporting from
   - ☐ a) a radio station in Washington, DC.
   - ☐ b) his mum's neighborhood.
   - ☐ c) from a parking lot.

2. Sonari Glinton introduces Dorothy Glinton as
   - ☐ a) a reporter of 30 years.
   - ☐ b) an experienced cook.
   - ☐ c) a daily shopper.

3. Dorothy Glinton made her pot roasts
   - ☐ a) while doing housework.
   - ☐ b) while helping in their shop.
   - ☐ c) after finishing the chores.

4. Dorothy Glinton often eats prepared food in
   - ☐ a) a fast food place.
   - ☐ b) a supermarket.
   - ☐ c) a salad bar.

5. Restaurant industry analyst Bonnie Riggs specifies that
   - ☐ a) people's concerns about dinner vary.
   - ☐ b) groceraunts prepare meals at the table.
   - ☐ c) Mariano's is a groceraunt.

6. Bonnie Riggs
   - ☐ a) visits countless old-fashioned restaurants.
   - ☐ b) cooks less than she used to.
   - ☐ c) is an organic food fan.

7. Elliott Silver and Noah Ellis from Picnic LA restaurant in Beverly Hills
   - ☐ a) opened up a luxury dining hall.
   - ☐ b) took exclusive red medicine.
   - ☐ c) imitated the restaurant they loved to eat at.

8. Silver and Ellis
   - ☐ a) approve of high labor costs.
   - ☐ b) grow their own organic vegetables.
   - ☐ c) employ just six people at Picnic LA.

9. Picnic LA
   - ☐ a) has set standards for some years now.
   - ☐ b) relies on high-end service standards.
   - ☐ c) is low-priced with regard to its high standards.

10. The people of the online service Blue Apron
    - ☐ a) prove their culinary skills on a daily basis.
    - ☐ b) prepare their meals in their own kitchens.
    - ☐ c) provide necessary ingredients for your meals.

11. Bonnie Riggs regards the new services by GrubHub, AmazonFresh, and Uber as
    - ☐ a) an unreliable source of profit for traditional fast-food chains.
    - ☐ b) a unique development in the food delivery business.
    - ☐ c) a reliable source of support to restaurant operators.

Annotations for the interview: **asparagus** Spargel ● **fennel** Fenchel ● **GrubHub, AmazonFresh, and Uber** here: *Lieferservice-Firmen*

Course: _____ Date: _____ Name: _____

Listening

◎ **The online identity crisis**

MULTIPLE CHOICE

First listen to the introduction of a report about our online identities. Tick the correct answer. There is one example (0.) at the beginning.

0. The world's most famous fictional spy, James Bond,
   - ☐ a) lives across the River Thames.
   - ☐ b) has revealed his identity.
   - ☑ c) works for MI6.

1. The information people give away about themselves
   - ☐ a) exposes their most private secrets.
   - ☐ b) is very useful to marketing companies.
   - ☐ c) ignores privacy and security standards.

2. Strangers tracking one's online identity
   - ☐ a) bear the consequences of their actions.
   - ☐ b) have previously identified James Bond.
   - ☐ c) study your character traits.

MULTIPLE CHOICE

Now listen to two experts commenting on the future of our online identities for the report.
Tick the correct answer.

3. Digital citizens cannot avoid
   - ☐ a) spreading their digital DNA.
   - ☐ b) being monitored online.
   - ☐ c) storing data in the cloud.

4. When walking down the street without being online you
   - ☐ a) encourage others to talk to you.
   - ☐ b) keep your thoughts and feelings to yourself.
   - ☐ c) worry about engaging in a conversation with others.

5. When walking down the street using social media you
   - ☐ a) keep your online activities secret.
   - ☐ b) make all kinds of personal data available.
   - ☐ c) spontaneously show pictures of family and friends.

6. Professor of Law Neil Richards worries that a multitude of digital footprints are
   - ☐ a) not accessible for everybody.
   - ☐ b) left around the house.
   - ☐ c) created without our knowledge.

7. 'Ad(vertisement) networks' collect private data to
   - ☐ a) resell them to interested parties.
   - ☐ b) direct our attention towards familiar products.
   - ☐ c) redirect our attention to particular social network companies.

8. Social networks and even traditional construction companies
   - ☐ a) cleverly place ads in the aisles of department stores.
   - ☐ b) carefully track their ads on our phones.
   - ☐ c) precisely locate consumers inside stores.

9. Consumer behavior is analyzed to define
   - ☐ a) architectural designs of future shops.
   - ☐ b) necessary product lines.
   - ☐ c) company perspectives.

10. Our online identities reflect our changing
    - ☐ a) technological progress.
    - ☐ b) buying customs.
    - ☐ c) work out activities.

Autor: Michael Rybicki, Buchholz in der Nordheide

Course: _____ Date: _____ Name: _____

Mediation

You are taking part in the European Erasmus school project called "Pursuing personal dreams – someone who has made it". It aims at motivating young people to stay in school while pursuing their career ambitions. You are asked to hand in a short and coherent article of approximately 160 words about a celebrity who has "made it" in German society. You have come across this excerpt from the German Zeit Magazin *and have decided to use it for your contribution.*

Elyas M'Barek: »Es ist für mich bis heute eine große Genugtuung, meinen Namen auf Kinoplakaten zu lesen«

Ich träume sehr viel und intensiv. Meine Träume lösen heftige Gefühle in mir aus, haben aber scheinbar nichts mit meinem Alltag zu tun. Im realen Leben bin ich kein Träumer, stattdessen hatte ich
5 schon immer Ziele, die ich erreichen wollte. Als Jugendlicher hatte ich allerdings keine Vorbilder, und nur wenige Menschen haben an mich geglaubt. Viele in meinem Umfeld haben mir immer wieder zu verstehen gegeben, dass ich ein Versager sei und
10 aus mir nichts werden würde. Eine Zeit lang habe ich das auch geglaubt. Ich bin ständig von der Schule geflogen und habe mich herumgetrieben. Es hat etwas gedauert, bis ich verstanden habe, dass es wichtig ist, auf meine innere Stimme zu hören,
15 meinen Fähigkeiten zu vertrauen und nicht dem Urteil anderer. Es wäre schön, wenn ich in die Vergangenheit zurückreisen könnte, um meinem Teenager-Ich zu sagen: »Du musst keine Angst haben! Lass dich nicht verunsichern, du musst nicht
20 rebellieren, alles wird gut. So, wie du bist, bist du prima, du wirst es allen zeigen!« So eine Botschaft hätte ich damals gut gebrauchen können.

In meiner Anfangszeit als Schauspieler gab es kaum Rollen für mich, über Jahre hinweg. Ich habe
25 alibimäßig studiert, damit meine Eltern zufrieden waren und es nicht auffiel, dass ich nur herumsaß und wartete. Damals habe ich einen bekannten

Schauspielkollegen getroffen, ebenfalls mit Migrationshintergrund. Ich habe mich vorgestellt, ihm gesagt, dass ich auch Schauspieler werden wolle, 30 und ihn um Rat gefragt. Er hat nur gesagt: »Ändere sofort deinen Nachnamen, mit dem wirst du in Deutschland keinen Erfolg haben.« Was für ein Blödsinn, habe ich gedacht. Ich habe mich nicht beirren lassen und weiter daran geglaubt, dass ich 35 Erfolg haben kann, wenn ich zu mir selbst stehe. Daher ist es für mich bis heute eine große Genugtuung, meinen Namen unverändert auf Kinoplakaten zu lesen.

Aktuell habe ich keine beruflichen Pläne. Im 40 Gegenteil, ich möchte das Erlebte wirken lassen, mein Leben und den Erfolg genießen, für den ich hart gearbeitet habe. Das geht nicht, wenn man im Kopf ständig mit den nächsten Projekten beschäftigt ist – dann kommen die schlechten Träume. Aber darüber 45 muss ich mir jetzt nicht den Kopf zerbrechen. […]

Einen großen Traum habe ich doch noch. Ich träume davon, dass es bald egal sein wird, was für einen Nachnamen man hat, wo man geboren wurde oder woher die Eltern kommen. Ich bin in 50 Deutschland geboren und aufgewachsen, die deutsche Kultur ist mein Zuhause, ich musste nie integriert werden. Das sollte eigentlich gar kein Thema sein.

(424 words)
Jörg Bockem, *Die Zeit*, 2017

Elyas M'Barek
Schauspieler (geb. 1982), wurde bekannt durch die Fernsehserie Türkisch für Anfänger und dem Kinofilm *Fuck ju Göhte*.

Autor: Michael Rybicki, Buchholz in der Nordheide
Textquelle: Jörg Böckem, www.zeit.de, 2017
Bildquelle: Getty Images (Christian Marquardt), München

Course: _____   Date: _____   Name: _____

Writing

Being cool

M1

"Explain to us, son, how gaining nine A levels is uncool and damages your street cred."

cred credibility; quality of being trustworthy and convincing

M2

to move on to make progress

M3: Characteristics of anti-social behaviour:
1. aggressiveness and/or violent behaviour
2. deception of others and misleading behaviour
3. impulsiveness and recklessness
4. ignorance of what is morally right
5. disregard for the rights of others
6. conflicts with the law

M4: Characteristics of maturity
1. controlling immediate wishes and desires
2. postponing the fulfilment of desires
3. thoughtfulness and sensitivity towards others
4. resistance to the influence of peers

1 *Describe one of the two cartoons (M1 or M2) and point out its message in a coherent text.*

2 *Choose either a), b) or c):*
a) *Examine which of the characteristics of anti-social behaviour (M3) apply to the first-person narrator in the short story "Chalk" by Meg Kearney. Write a coherent text of about 150 words.*

OR

b) *Examine which of the characteristics of anti-social behaviour (M3) apply to Seth's friend Adam in the short story "On the bridge" by Todd Strasser. Write a coherent text of about 150 words.*

OR

c) *Examine which characteristics of maturity (M4) apply to Seth at the end of the short story "On the bridge" by Todd Strasser. Write a coherent text of about 150 words.*

3 *"It takes courage to grow up and become who you really are."*
(E. E. Cummings, American author, 1894–1962).
Write a personal comment on Cummings's statement and refer to your findings in tasks 1 and 2 and to one of the short stories read in class.

Autor: Michael Rybicki, Buchholz in der Nordheide
Textquelle: E. E. Cummings, quoted in Enormous Smallness: a story of E.E. Cummings, Enchanted Lion Books, 2015
Bildquellen: 1. www.CartoonStock.com (mtun567), Bath; 2. www.CartoonStock.com (Hill, Spencer), Bath

Course: _____   Date: _____   Name: _____

Reading and writing

Personality, privacy and our digital selves

It used to be that only very important things were written down. The deeds of kings, the titles to land and the stories of the saints. For the rest of us, the most that we could expect was for our lives to be
5 noted on tax surveys and tombstones.

In contrast, almost everything we do today leaves a digital trace. […] Soon our whole lives will in principle (if not in fact) be archived in minute detail, with increasingly limited ability to opt out. What is a
10 boon[1] for some future historians should cause concerns for us.

What are we to make of this digital footprint? How should we feel about such levels of transparency and archiving of our lives? Luckily for us, the
15 fragmentation of our tools, and the changing fashions between applications and formats means that there isn't a master algorithm that relates all of these information into a seamless whole. […]

However, all of this may change if the marriage of
20 the science of personality and our digital behaviour becomes a fact of life. Forget the long personality quizzes and cookie-cutter personality types. Abilities to extract personality from our digital behaviour and infer who we are, predicting how we'll behave, is
25 much closer than we think.

The implications of this advance could be momentous, for personality is the glue that could unite our fragmented digital traces into rich portraits of ourselves, allowing those who hold a digital
30 fragment to infer us whole and entire. […]

While the algorithms, profit models and actors in this space are fluid and unfolding, we can assume with some certainty that in the future our digital selves will have personalities that are accessible to anyone
35 who cares to look. These will be more revealing than a conversation with us, and more accurate than our

own hopes and desires. It will be, possibly, an age of true digital transparency.

What sort of world will this be? Here we can offer a Manichean[2] thought experiment in the form of 40 two scenarios.

In the first scenario, our digital selves are outside of our control. Our personal data is owned by the hardware and software we use, and sold to the highest bidder. Anonymity and privacy are in demand 45 but very expensive – there is no feasible opt-out clause. In this world our every engagement with the digital world creates food for marketing and social engineering of Orwellian[3] proportions. Here we are talking about the fundamental loss of agency, a world 50 in which our individuality is used as fodder for consumption and manipulation. When Socrates[4] exhorted us to "know thyself", it is doubtful he ever entertained the possibility that we may live in a world where others know us better than we can know 55 ourselves, and use that knowledge to take over our agency.

In the second scenario, we retain the right to our personal data and carefully monitor who can use it and for what purpose. In this sense, our digital selves 60 become our agents and avatars, revealing our preferences for specific purposes we've assigned to them, but without ability to be used obliquely against us. We'll have as many digital selves as required, ensuring that their fragmentation works for us instead 65 of against us. And, where useful, we'll use the personality of our digital selves for both self-insight and growth, helping us lead more authentic lives but preventing others from using this information to manipulate or game us. 70

(574 words)

Dave Winsborough, Darko Lovric and Tomas
Chamorro-Premuzic et al., *The Guardian*, 2016

---

1 boon sth that makes life better or easier ● **2 Manichean** a simplified way of looking at the world that classifies everything as either good or evil ● **3 Orwellian** of or like the society portrayed by Orwell (real name Eric Arthur Blair, 1903–50) in his novel *1984*, in which a totalitarian state exercises almost total control over the public and private activities of its citizens ● **4 Socrates** Greek philosopher (around 400 BC)

1   COMPREHENSION
Outline the author's ideas about how our online footprint may affect us in the future.

2   ANALYSIS
Examine how the author of the article draws the reader's interest and keeps him/her reading.

Course: _____ **Date:** _____ **Name:** _____

3   EVALUATION

Choose one of the following tasks (include information you received in class as well):

a) *Which of the two scenarios depicted in the article (ll. 39ff.) do you find more likely to occur? Give reasons.*

OR

b) *"In the future our digital selves will have personalities that are accessible to anyone who cares to look"*
    (ll. 33–35). Write a letter to the editor in which you comment on the statement.

Reading

SENTENCE COMPLETION

Read the text and then complete the following sentences.

1. In the past only the actions of VIPs such as royals and saints were written down because _____

    _____

2. Nowadays it is almost impossible to remain anonymous because _____

    _____

3. We are not completely transparent yet because _____

    _____

4. Any piece of digital information about us on the internet is of great use to people/organisations because

    _____

5. The future could be an age of true digital transparency because _____

    _____

6. In the first scenario we will have no influence on our data because _____

    _____

7. We probably won't be able to remain anonymous because _____

    _____

8. Socrates' dictum is no longer valid because _____

    _____

9. The fact that we have multiple digital selves in the second scenario is positive because _____

    _____

10. The second scenario is much less dystopian because _____

    _____

11. The second scenario is more challenging for us because _____

    _____

Autor: Ralf Kerstgens, Münster

Course: _____   Date: _____   Name: _____

Reading and writing

The Circle by Dave Eggers

Mae opened the intra-company stream and began. She was determined to get through all the Inner and Outer feeds that night. […] She plowed through the messages, every one, looking for anything she would
5 have reasonably been expected to answer personally. There were surveys, at least 50 of them, gauging[1] the Circlers' opinions on various company policies, on optimal dates for upcoming gatherings, interest groups, celebrations and holiday breaks. There were
10 dozens of clubs soliciting members and notifying all of meetings: there were cat-owner groups – at least 10 – a few rabbit groups, six reptile groups, four of them adamantly[2] snake-exclusive. Most of all, there were groups for dog-owners. She counted 22, but was sure
15 that wasn't all of them. One of the groups dedicated to the owners of very small dogs, Lucky Lapdogs, wanted to know how many people would join a weekend club for walks and hikes and support; Mae ignored this one. Then, realising that ignoring it would only prompt a
20 second, more urgent, message, she typed a message, explaining that she didn't have a dog. She was asked to sign a petition for more vegan options at lunch; she did. There were nine messages from various work-groups within the company, asking her to join their
25 subCircles for more specific updates and information sharing. For now she joined the ones dedicated to crochet, soccer, and Hitchcock.

By 10pm, she'd made her way through all the intra-company messages and alerts, and now turned
30 to her own OuterCircle account. She hadn't visited in six days, and found 118 new notices from that day alone. She decided to plow through, newest to oldest.

Most recently, one of her friends from college had posted a message about having the stomach flu[3], and a long thread followed, with friends making 35 suggestions about remedies, some offering sympathy, some posting photos meant to cheer her up. Mae liked two of the photos, liked three of the comments, posted her own well wishes, and sent a link to a song, "Puking Sally", that she'd found. That prompted a new thread, 40 54 notices, about the song and the band that wrote it. One of the friends on the thread said he knew the bassist in the band, and then looped him into the conversation. The bassist, Damien Ghilotti, was in New Zealand, was a studio engineer now, but was happy to 45 know that "Puking Sally" was still resonating with the flu-ridden. His post thrilled all involved, and another 129 notices appeared, everyone thrilled to hear from the actual bassist from the band, and by the end of the thread, Damien Ghilotti was invited to play a wedding, 50 if he wanted, or visit Boulder, or Bath, or Gainesville, or St Charles, Illinois, any time he happened to be passing through, and he would have a place to stay and a home-cooked meal. Upon the mention of St Charles, someone asked if anyone from there had 55 heard about Tim Jenkins, who was fighting in Afghanistan; they'd seen some mention of a kid from Illinois being shot to death by an Afghan insurgent[4] posing as a police officer. Sixty messages later the respondents had determined that it was a different Tim 60 Jenkins, this one from Rantoul, Illinois, not St Charles. There was relief all around […] and Mae, feeling some darkness opening its wings within her, signed off.

(560 words)

From: Dave Eggers, *The Circle,* 2013

1 to gauge to measure ● **2 adamantly** strictly ● **3 flu** short for influenza ● **4 insurgent** rebel

1   COMPREHENSION
Summarise how Mae deals with her feeds.

2   ANALYSIS
Analyse how Eggers criticises the use of streaming services.

3   EVALUATION
a) *Comment on the following proposal: Every internet user should only be allowed to join a certain number of clubs on the internet.*

OR

b) *Imagine you are Damien Ghilotti. Write a diary entry after he has gone through the whole thread concerning the song his band wrote.*

Autor: Ralf Kerstgens, Münster

Textquelle: Excerpt(s) from THE CIRCLE by Dave Eggers, copyright © 2013 by Dave Eggers. Used by permission of Alfred A. Knopf, an imprint of the Knopf Doubleday Publishing Group, a division of Penguin Random House LLC. All rights reserved. Any third party use of this material, outside of this publication, is prohibited. Interested parties must apply directly to Penguin Random House LLC for permission.

Course: _____ Date: _____ Name: _____

Reading

MULTIPLE CHOICE
Read the text, then tick the correct answer. Only one answer is correct.

1. Some of the surveys in Mae's feed wanted to know what the Circlers thought about
   - ☐ a) the best times to meet.
   - ☐ b) pet insurance policies.
   - ☐ c) dating other employees.
   - ☐ d) other people's profiles.

2. How many clubs are mentioned in the text?
   - ☐ a) 5
   - ☐ b) 10
   - ☐ c) 22
   - ☐ d) about 48

3. Mae decided to leave a message on "Lucky Lapdogs" because she
   - ☐ a) does not like hikes.
   - ☐ b) does not have a dog.
   - ☐ c) wants to show her support for the club.
   - ☐ d) does not want to receive or write another message.

4. Which clubs does Mae join?
   - ☐ a) Vegan Club
   - ☐ b) SubCircle Club
   - ☐ c) The Football Club
   - ☐ d) The Film Club

5. She had dealt with all intra-company messages and alerts
   - ☐ a) until after midnight.
   - ☐ b) before 10 at night.
   - ☐ c) after 10 at night.
   - ☐ d) at 10 in the morning.

6. She started with the following Outer-Circle messages:
   - ☐ a) the long ones.
   - ☐ b) the short ones.
   - ☐ c) the most recent ones.
   - ☐ d) the oldest ones.

7. In the stomach flu thread the following contents can be found:
   - ☐ a) condolences.
   - ☐ b) comments.
   - ☐ c) websites.
   - ☐ d) emojis.

8. Damien Ghilotti gets the following offers:
   - ☐ a) to play at a festival.
   - ☐ b) to get a free meal in a restaurant in Bath.
   - ☐ c) to marry.
   - ☐ d) a place to spend the night while travelling.

9. The "real" Tim Jenkins comes from
   - ☐ a) St. Charles.
   - ☐ b) Afghanistan.
   - ☐ c) Rantoul.
   - ☐ d) Gainesville.

10. Mae signed off feeling
    - ☐ a) frustrated.
    - ☐ b) happy.
    - ☐ c) proud.
    - ☐ d) tired.

11. There was relief all around at the end of the stream of messages because
    - ☐ a) they could all go to sleep.
    - ☐ b) nobody had to think about war any longer.
    - ☐ c) nobody liked St Charles.
    - ☐ d) they had written their daily share of messages.

12. When she goes to bed Mae has read
    - ☐ a) only the Inner-Circle feeds.
    - ☐ b) only the Outer-Circle feeds.
    - ☐ c) all the Inner-and Outer-Circle messages.
    - ☐ d) only the ones that she had to answer personally.

Course: _____ Date: _____ Name: _____

Listening

 **Religion in a Digital Age**

MULTIPLE CHOICE
Listen to an interview with a priest, Dr Pete Phillips, and tick the correct answer. Only one answer is correct.

1. At which university can you find the CODEC research centre?
   - ☐ a) Derby
   - ☐ b) Derry
   - ☐ c) Durham
   - ☐ d) Fulham

2. Why is Pete Phillips a remarkable priest?
   - ☐ a) he lives in on a university campus
   - ☐ b) he has founded CODEC
   - ☐ c) he teaches digital culture and theology
   - ☐ d) he uses new technologies

3. How many aspects of spirituality can be downloaded onto your smartphone?
   - ☐ a) two
   - ☐ b) many
   - ☐ c) a few
   - ☐ d) only mindfulness

4. What are people asked to do when they bring their phones to church?
   - ☐ a) to put them in silent mode
   - ☐ b) to turn them off
   - ☐ c) to put them in flight mode
   - ☐ d) to hand them over

5. Why is it a good thing to use apps during mass?
   - ☐ a) people can communicate easily
   - ☐ b) the priest has more control
   - ☐ c) parents can check on their children
   - ☐ d) the priest can connect better to the congregation[1]

6. According to Dr Phillips, what has Christianity always been good at?
   - ☐ a) adapting to modern times and conditions
   - ☐ b) convincing people
   - ☐ c) keeping its rituals and ceremonies
   - ☐ d) changing people

7. What will Christianity focus on in the future?
   - ☐ a) marketing
   - ☐ b) helping minorities
   - ☐ c) connecting people online
   - ☐ d) selling religious objects online

8. Why do many denominations[2] find it difficult to accept online sacraments[3]?
   - ☐ a) they don't like online adverts
   - ☐ b) there is no real communion[4]
   - ☐ c) they don't want their children online
   - ☐ d) not everyone has access to the internet

9. Which church published a huge survey on "Online Sacraments"?
   - ☐ a) Catholic
   - ☐ b) Anglican
   - ☐ c) Methodist
   - ☐ d) Protestant

10. Why does Dr Phillips think online sacraments are possible?
    - ☐ a) the Internet is fast enough today
    - ☐ b) you can have community online
    - ☐ c) social media is widespread
    - ☐ d) other things can be linked to online

11. What has CODEC discovered about how people are using the bible on social media?
    - ☐ a) a change in the apps used
    - ☐ b) more Jesus quote shares
    - ☐ c) a decrease in the number of shares
    - ☐ d) more shares of warm-hearted verses

● **1 congregation** people attending a church service ● **2 denomination** a particular religious group which has slightly different beliefs from other groups within the same faith, e.g. Catholics or Protestants ● **3 sacrament** a Christian religious ceremony such as communion, baptism or marriage ● **4 communion** Christian ceremony in which people eat bread and drink wine in memory of Christ's death

Autor: Ralf Kerstgens, Münster

Course: _____ **Date:** _____ **Name:** _____

Listening

 Free Wi-Fi is coming to New York City

SENTENCE COMPLETION
Listen to the report and then complete the following sentences.

1. The spread of mobile phones across America has led to _____

    _____

2. Pay phones are being replaced by _____

    _____

3. The _LinkNYC_ program is expected to install _____

    _____

4. _Citybridge_ is an alliance of _____ companies and one of them, Intersection,

    is owned by Alphabet, which _____

    _____

5. New York City will pay for the program and is optimistic to profit from the links through _____

    _____

6. _____ will be covered by Wi-Fi.

7. Wi-Fi speeds are _____ faster than home networks.

8. To access the secure network, users have to register with their email account and _____

    _____

9. In case of an emergency, citizens _____

    _____

10. Because the kiosks have cameras they will make it easier to record (2 items) _____

    _____

    and _____

11. If you live near such a kiosk, _____

12. Two aspects concerning privacy issues that may be seen as critical are _____

    _____

    and _____

13. The report is useful for people who are looking forward to using free Wi-Fi because (_one item_) _____

    _____

Course: _____   Date: _____   Name: _____

Mediation

You are doing a project on the positive and negative effects of social media on families with a partner school in Geraldine, New Zealand. Write a blog entry for St. Geraldine High School's website which outlines the opportunities and dangers of Whatsapp according to Corinna Berghahn's article in the Neue Osnabrücker Zeitung.

Fluch oder Segen? Whatsapp, Facebook, Skype in Familien

Der Microsoft-Dienst Skype oder sein Apple Pendant werden von Familien vor allem dann genutzt, wenn die Kinder außer Haus sind – ob als Erwachsene oder in einem Austauschjahr, erklärt die freie
5 Medienpädagogin Susanne Häring.

Alltäglicher ist jedoch der Gebrauch von Messenger-Apps wie Whatsapp: Der Sohn verspätet sich mit dem Zug? Per Smartphone kann er den Eltern Bescheid geben, sodass sie sich am Bahnhof nicht
10 die Beine in den Bauch stehen müssen. Und dauerblockierte Telefone? Dank Smartphones sind Jugendliche inzwischen fast permanent mit Gleichaltrigen im kommunikativen Austausch und Kontakt, ohne dass sie noch das Telefon der Eltern
15 benutzen müssen.

Doch nicht nur mit den Freunden: Bei Whatsapp lässt sich kinderleicht eine Gruppe erstellen, viele Familien nutzen dieses auch für Familiengruppen. Nie war es daher so einfach, dass Großeltern, Eltern und Kinder
20 an einem Chat teilnehmen, Nachrichten austauschen und sich schnell Bilder zuschicken können. Selbst Aufforderungen wie „Räum Dein Zimmer auf" erreichen nun auch die Kinder, die in Zeiten der Pubertät lieber ganz aus dem Blickfeld der Eltern
25 entschwinden. Kurzum: Die digitale Kommunikation erschafft Nähe, erzeugt aber auch Kontrolle.

Häring […] sieht das ähnlich: „Wenn sich beide Seiten auf die Nutzung moderner Kommunikationsmittel einlassen, ist es eine schöne

Sache: Informationen können schnell geteilt, 30
Emotionen per Bildchen dargestellt und Fotos zugeschickt werden." Die Welt – und Familie – rückt im besten Falle also zusammen.

Im weniger guten Fall können sich Kinder jedoch auch durch ihre Eltern kontrolliert fühlen: Bei 35
Whatsapp ist es beispielsweise möglich zu sehen, wann ein Nutzer zuletzt online war und ob eine Nachricht gelesen wurde: „Warum hast Du nicht sofort auf meine Nachricht geantwortet? Ich sehe doch, dass Du sie gelesen hast", ist so auch eine der 40
häufigen Fragen, die besorgte Eltern an ihre Kinder richten. […]

Knackpunkt ist jedoch auch das Unwissen vieler Nutzer über die Hintergründe moderner Kommunikationswege: „Facebook ist für viele böse, 45
Whatsapp jedoch praktisch. Doch Eltern realisieren genauso wenig wie ihre Kinder, dass Facebook, Whatsapp und Instagram ein und derselbe Konzern sind – und dass sie die Rechte an ihren bei vermeintlich nur in der privaten Chat-Gruppe 50
gesendeten Bilder immer an diesen einen Konzern abtreten. Theoretisch könnte der mit den Bildern die Litfaßsäulen aller Länder plakatieren." Was Häring rät: „Die AGBs lesen. Und immer im Kopf behalten, dass Whatsapp, Facebook und Co. nicht kostenlos 55
sind, sondern mit unseren Daten bezahlt werden."

(387 Wörter)
Corinna Berghahn, *Neue Osnabrücker Zeitung*, 2015

Course: _____　Date: _____　Name: _____

Writing

Digital Trail

1　*Describe the cartoon.*

2　*Analyse the message of the cartoon.*

3　*Comment on the message of the cartoon.*

Writing

High School Students' Views on their Digital Footprint

Digital Footprint Actions	Gender		Community Type		
	Girls	Boys	Urban	Sub	Rural
I am careful about posting and texting information about myself or others.	52 %	41 %	46 %	44 %	48 %
I have advised friends to not post certain things about me or others.	34 %	25 %	30 %	28 %	30 %
I have stopped interacting with someone based upon their online profile.	29 %	20 %	24 %	23 %	26 %
I use digital footprints to find people to connect with.	12 %	12 %	13 %	12 %	12 %
I think it is important to have a positive online profile.	38 %	27 %	32 %	31 %	33 %

1　*Sum up the statistics on digital footprint actions provided in the table.*

2　*Analyse the influence of gender and community in the table. In doing so, also consider explanations and consequences.*

3　a) *Write a letter to your project partner at a US high school in which you comment on the internet use and the digital footprint actions in the table.*

　　OR

　　b) *Comment on the following quote:*
　　"If there is one modern catchphrase that all of us should take to heart in this matter, it's this: The internet is forever." (David Bohl/Brad Pasley)

Autor: Ralf Kerstgens, Münster
Textquellen: 1. © Project Tomorrow 2014; 2. David B. Bohl, http://www.slowdownfast.com
Bildquelle: www.CartoonStock.com (Slane, Chris), Bath

Course: _____ Date: _____ Name: _____

Reading and writing

Seven dirty words, according to the Trump administration

WORDS ARE power. Whether used to twist or reveal, language matters, especially that used by the people who govern a nation devoted to free speech. This is why it was such a shock to hear the Department of
5 Health and Human Services (*HSS*) instruct some of its divisions, including the Centers for Disease Control and Prevention (*CDC*), to avoid using certain words or phrases in official documents being drafted for next year's budget. It sounds like thought police at
10 work.

If that judgment seems harsh, consider what happens in China, where thought police really exist. China routinely censors articles containing politically sensitive words such as "Taiwan," "Tibet" and "cultur-
15 al revolution" from publications because it does not want its people to think about them. Writing about democracy could lead to trouble in Belarus[1], Cuba or Vietnam, too. In Russia, words that refer to gays positively can trigger a penalty. In Saudi Arabia, a
20 blogger, Raif Badawi, sits in jail for his online appeal for a more liberal and secular society.

It is not a far stretch from these examples of misguided censorship abroad to the actions of the HHS[2] language militia. According to *Post* reporters Lena H.
25 Sun and Juliet Eilperin, policy types at the CDC[3] in Atlanta were told of the list of forbidden terms at a meeting Dec. 14 during a 90-minute briefing to discuss the upcoming budget request. The terms prohibited to use are: "vulnerable," "entitlement,"
30 "diversity," "transgender," "fetus," "evidence-based" and "science-based." They also reported that in some cases, the policy folks[4] were given alternatives; instead of "science-based" or "evidence-based," the

suggested phrase is "CDC bases its recommenda-
35 tions on science in consideration with community standards and wishes." But in other cases, no replacement words were immediately offered.

The CDC's new director, Brenda Fitzgerald, replied that "there are no banned words at CDC."
40 That's a relief, given the agency's mission, which includes acting as sentinel for public health, warning of threats and responding rapidly to meet them. But Ms. Fitzgerald's assurance does not ease concerns that higher-ups[5] at HHS are insisting on banned
45 words to enforce a political and ideological agenda. Why would they eliminate "vulnerable," "entitlement," "diversity" and "transgender" in a budget document other than to airbrush the ideas out of the underlying policy?

50 Just as distressing is the attempt to limit the use of "evidence-based" and "science-based." Unfettered scientific research is vital for maintaining public health, even when the results are unpopular with some communities and points of view. Being
55 able to talk about science is absolutely critical in, say, understanding the value of childhood vaccination in preventing the spread of measles. "Fetus" is a scientific word essential to exploring the impact of the Zika virus on the health of infants and pregnant wom-
60 en. And can there be an honest discussion of the health effects of climate change without science and evidence? Does anyone gain by hiding the truth these words express? No. Someone should tell the foolish thought police at HHS to stand down.

(506 words)

By the Editorial Board of the *Washington Post*, 2018

---

1 **Belarus** *Weißrussland* ● 2 **HHS** Department of Health and Human Services ● 3 **CDC** Centers for Disease Control and Prevention ● 4 **policy folks** high-ranking politicians ● 5 **higher-ups** high-ranking executives

1 COMPREHENSION
Outline in your own words the main concerns the board raises and the intended message of the text.

2 ANALYSIS
Analyse how the authors convey their message.

3 EVALUATION
In a letter to the editor comment on the board's views.

Course: _____ Date: _____ Name: _____

Reading

TRUE OR FALSE?

Read the text. Are the statements true or false? Tick the correct box and give the line numbers and the first and last three words of the quote from the text to support your answers. There is one example (0):

	TRUE	FALSE
0. Language is a strong tool for explaining or hiding the truth. l./ll.: <u>Words are power … devoted to free speech.</u>	✓	
1. The skilful use of language is essential for politicians. l./ll.: _____		
2. The HHS is accused of taking advantage of its power. l./ll.: _____		
3. Countries like China try particularly hard to keep its language open and free. l./ll.: _____		✓
4. In some countries people are imprisoned for using their right of free speech. l./ll.: <u>In Saudi Arabia, a blogger ,…., sits in jail</u> *for his online appeal for a more liberal and secular society* ✓		
5. The authors relate the restrictions to free speech in some countries to current tendencies in the USA. l./ll.: _____		
6. Spokespeople of the CDC were told to rephrase their public statements to avoid the claim that science or facts were elementary to the process. l./ll.: _____		
7. Brenda Fitzgerald denies the influence of political pressure. l./ll.: _____		
8. Fitzgerald's statement comes as a relief to the author of the newspaper article. l./ll.: _____		
9. Forbidding certain expressions is an attempt to change political thought. l./ll.: _____		
10. Restricting science is dangerous. l./ll.: _____		
11. There is doubt that the work of the 'thought police' at HSS is beneficial. l./ll.: _____		

Course: _____   Date: _____   Name: _____

Reading and writing

Nullen   Kreuze

Noughts and Crosses by Malorie Blackman

Persephone ("Sephy") Hadley is a 'Cross'; she has dark skin and is the daughter of a wealthy senior politician, Kamal Hadley. Callum McGregor is a 'Nought' with light skin. In their world Noughts and Crosses simply don't mix.

The train journey from hell, that's what it was. A journey which ruined the rest of the day as far as I was concerned.

5 We were on our way to Celebration Park. There were only three more stops to go when they got on. Police officers on a routine inspection. Two of them, boredom plastered over their faces.

'ID passes please. ID passes please.'
Sephy looked surprised. I wasn't. We both dug out
10 our ID cards as they made their way up the first-class train carriage. I watched the cursory glances they gave the ID passes of all the Crosses in the carriage. I was the only Nought. Would they stop and ask me lots of questions? Huh! Is pig poo smelly?

15 An officer of trim build and sporting a pencil-thin moustache stood right in front of me. He looked at me, then took my ID pass without a word. (…)

The officer looked from my ID card to my face and back again. My thumbprint was on the card. Was
20 he going to break out a magnifying glass and ask me to hold out my right hand so he could compare the imprint on the card to my print? It wouldn't've surprised me.

'You're a long way from home, boy.'
25 I bit down on the inside of my bottom lip, not trusting myself to speak. Both officious officials stood in front of me now. There was barely enough room to get a paperclip between their legs and my knees. I sighed.(…)
30 'Let me see your ticket.'
I handed it over.
'Where did you get the money to buy this kind of ticket?'
I looked up at them, but didn't speak. What was
35 there to say? They had the scent of blood in their nostrils and I didn't stand a chance, no matter what I said or did. So why bother?

'I asked you a question,' Moustache reminded me. As if I'd forgotten.
40 'Did you buy this ticket?' Moustache's accomplice asked.

The truth or prevarication? What was Sephy thinking? I couldn't see her. The no-brain brothers were in the way. If only I could see her face.

'I asked you a question, boy. Did you buy this   45
ticket?'
'No, I didn't,' I replied.
'Come with us, please.'
Time to get my posterior pummelled. Time to get
my derriere dealt with. Time to get my bum bounced   50
right off the train.

How dare a Nought sit in first class? It's outrageous. It's a scandal. It's disgusting. Disinfect that seat at once.

'Officer, he's with me. I bought the tickets.' Sephy   55
was on her feet. 'Is there a problem?'
'And you are?'
'Persephone Hadley. My dad's the Home Office Minister, Kamal Hadley. Callum is my friend,' Sephy said firmly.   60
'He is?'
'Yes, he is.' Sephy's voice had a steely tone to it that I'd never heard before. Not from her anyway.
'I see,' said Moustache.
'I can give you my father's private phone number.   65
I'm sure he'll sort all this out in a moment. Or you'll be able to talk to Juno Ayelette, his personal secretary.' Careful, Sephy. I'm tripping over all those names you're dropping.
'So is there a problem, Officer?' repeated Sephy.   70
Sniff! Sniff! Was I imagining things or was there the definite hint of a threat in the air? And I wasn't the only one to smell it. Moustache handed back my ID pass.
'Would you like to see my ID as well?' Sephy   75
held out her pass.
'That won't be necessary, Miss Hadley.' Moustache almost bowed. (…)
I turned to look out of the window. I didn't want to look at Sephy. Not yet. I didn't want to blame her for   80
the way the police treated me and every other Nought I knew. (…)I didn't want to resent Sephy for the way my education was automatically assumed to be less important than hers. I didn't want to hate her because she was a Cross and different to me. So I carried on   85
looking out of the window, pushing the knot of loathing deeper inside me. Deeper and deeper.

(718 words)
From: Malorie Blackman, *Noughts and Crosses*, 2001

Autor: Hartmut Klose,Seevetal
Textquelle: From: "Noughts and Crosses", by Malorie Blackman, Corgi Books (Random House Children's Books), London, 2006.

Course: _____ **Date:** _____ **Name:** _____

1   COMPREHENSION
Outline the changes in Callum's emotions.

2   ANALYSIS
Examine how the author characterises Sephy.

3   EVALUATION
Discuss which of the people in this scene oversteps borders.

Reading

SHORT ANSWERS
Read the text and then answer the questions in 1-8 words.

1. How does Callum perceive the emotional state of the officers?

    _____

2. How does Callum feel when the officers approach him?

    _____

3. How does the officer check Callum's identity?

    _____

4. What attitude does the officer reveal with his first direct statement to Callum?

    _____

5. Why do the officers stand so close to Callum?

    _____

6. Why does Callum not answer any questions?

    _____

7. What does Callum expect to happen?

    _____

8. What does Callum think he has done wrong?

    _____

9. How does Sephy act towards the officers?

    _____

10. What is Mustache's major concern?

    _____

11. What is Callum's emotional reaction towards the inequality he has had to face again?

    _____

Listening

◉ **U.S. Bakeries Grab A Slice Of A Latin American Tradition: Three Kings Cake**

MULTIPLE CHOICE
You will hear an interview about roscas de reyes, traditional and very popular Latino Christmas cakes. Tick the correct answer.

1. The broadcaster is talking about a special event in Los Angeles where people can
    ☐ a) meet the King of Spain.
    ☐ b) learn to bake a cake.
    ☐ c) make *roscas de reyes* together.
    ☐ d) see a huge *rosca de reyes*.

2. In the baking process, the *roscas*
    ☐ a) change their colour and become more appealing.
    ☐ b) become wet and sticky.
    ☐ c) are turned upside down.
    ☐ d) change into a lush dark color.

3. "La Mexicana bakery" in Alexandria was opened in
    ☐ a) 2002.
    ☐ b) 2005.
    ☐ c) 2010.
    ☐ d) 2012.

4. The person who finds the small figurine of the baby Jesus
    ☐ a) will have good luck next year.
    ☐ b) will have to throw a party.
    ☐ c) will have to bring *roscas* next year.
    ☐ d) has to drink a glass of tequila.

5. The dough of the *roscas de reyes*
    ☐ a) is sugar-free.
    ☐ b) is made with anise extract.
    ☐ c) takes 30 minutes to bake.
    ☐ d) is made with a lot of cocoa.

6. The cakes are oval-shaped because
    ☐ a) they fit better into the oven.
    ☐ b) they represent a king.
    ☐ c) they represent the baby Jesus.
    ☐ d) they represent a crown.

7. Pati Jinich is enthusiastic about *roscas* because
    ☐ a) she made them on her TV show.
    ☐ b) she has just opened a bakery.
    ☐ c) she has known about them since she was a child.
    ☐ d) she is very religious.

8. The *roscas* became more and more popular in the US, because
    ☐ a) the American children love them.
    ☐ b) the Latino community is growing.
    ☐ c) the Catholic included them into their services.
    ☐ d) many Latin American countries were colonized.

9. How many *roscas* did Tony Salazar sell the first time he made them?
    ☐ a) Less than 20
    ☐ b) 50–100
    ☐ c) 100–1,000
    ☐ d) over 5,000

10. It's not only families who order *roscas de reyes*, but also
    ☐ a) schools and companies.
    ☐ b) schools and kindergartens.
    ☐ c) companies and local authorities.
    ☐ d) schools and local authorities.

11. The report's main topic is about
    ☐ a) healthy food.
    ☐ b) food and culture.
    ☐ c) start-up bakeries.
    ☐ d) Mexican immigrants.

Autor: Hartmut Klose,Seevetal

Course: _____ Date: _____ Name: _____

Listening

 ***Sesame Street* in education programs**

SENTENCE COMPLETION
Introduction: Listen to the interview with Sherrie Westin and complete the following sentences with 1–5 words.

0. Example: Sherrie Westin is part of a team that wants to change *the lives of millions of children.*

1. The MacArthur Foundation granted the makers of *Sesame Street* $100 million to develop _____

    _____ for Syrian refugees.

SENTENCE COMPLETION
Main part: Complete the following sentences with 1–7 words each.

1. The *Sesame Street* puppets live through difficult situations that _____

    _____

2. Sherrie Westin's team wants to reach the children by *(name 2 ways)*_____

    _____

3. The majority of refugees live outside camps in *(name 1)* _____

4. Besides the mass broad reach, the individual touch is ensured by *(name 1)* _____

    _____

5. Children under five in particular may suffer lifelong psychological consequences that affect _____

    _____

6. The *Sesame Street* program wants to focus on the weakest refugees to give them _____

    _____

7. The professionals of Sesame Workshop go and meet a *(name 1)* _____

8. The MacArthur Grant finances professionals who visit families in order to _____

    _____

9. Parents are taught methods by those professionals to engage with their children with/by/in _____

    _____

10. The parents begin to understand that _____

    _____

11. With the support of the MacArthur Grant, the Sesame Workshop will be able to change the humanitarian

    response model for _____

Course: _____ Date: _____ Name: _____

Mediation

You are a member of the Teens4Teens organisation, which has asked you to report on views about the latest developments of opinion in Germany with regard to the refugee question. You have come across this article from the German newspaper Die Zeit, *which looks at central issues from various perspectives. In a blog post of about 180 words you present its positions.*

Flüchtlingsdebatte: Deutschland im Kreisverkehr

Völlig abgesehen davon, ob „wir", die deutschen Bürger, es schaffen, könnte man doch beginnen zu fragen: Schaffen die das?

Schaffen es die Flüchtlinge?

5 Wieso stellt sich diese Frage angesichts der immensen Verluste und des Leids, das die Geflohenen erfahren haben, in Deutschland zu keinem Zeitpunkt? Wieso dreht sich keine einzige deutsche Talkshow um die Perspektive der Geflohenen? Und

10 wieso wissen wir so wenig über die Lebensverhältnisse der Iraker, Afghanen und Syrer, wo sie doch zu Tausenden in unserem Land leben? Sie müssten unsere politischen Korrespondenten sein. Nur sie können detailliert berichten, was ihnen widerfuhr

15 und welche politischen Perspektiven sie sich für ihre Heimatländer vorstellen und wünschen.

Aber alles Spekulieren, Diskutieren und Politisieren geschieht aus der Sicht der Deutschen. Wir kreisen immer um uns. Es dreht sich stets um die

20 Angst, die "wir" vor "ihnen", den Fremden, haben. Um die Erschöpfung unserer Helfer. Um die Sorgen unserer Politiker. Um die Anstrengung unserer Kommunen. Um die Lösungen, die "wir" mit den Diktatoren vor Ort treffen müssen. Unsere Kapazitä-

25 ten, unsere Machbarkeit, unsere Ressourcen, kurz, wir, die Egogesellschaft, rücken uns ins Zentrum aller Debatten.

Die schutzsuchenden Asylbewerber sind in diesem Land darauf angewiesen, dass sie in der

30 Öffentlichkeit eine Stimme bekommen, die durch unermüdlichen Protest stellvertretend für sie um ein würdiges und gesundes Leben in Deutschland kämpft. Nichts ist selbstverständlich. Kein Brot, kein Wasser, kein beheiztes Zelt, keine Decken, keine

35 Medikamente. Es ist nicht der Staat, der die Flüchtlinge in Schutz nahm, sondern es waren die Bürger,

die im Widerstand zu einem nicht funktionierenden Staat dafür sorgten, dass es Notfallbetreuung und Erstversorgungen gab. Die politischen Parteien haben derzeit keinerlei Skrupel, sämtliche Bedenken 40 der rechtsradikalen Kräfte in ihre politischen Programme zu integrieren, aber sie haben immense Skrupel, in der Öffentlichkeit souverän aufzutreten und für die Sache der Flüchtlinge einzustehen. Die Folge sind weitere Asylrechtsverschärfungen an 45 einem Asylgesetz, das es eigentlich schon lange nicht mehr gibt. Es ist alles eine Frage der Perspektive. Im Moment gestaltet sich der Diskurs so, dass die Aufnahme der Flüchtlinge zähneknirschend erfolgt war, weshalb alles, was den Flüchtlingen zugute 50 kommt, wie Impfungen oder Schulpflicht, der Öffentlichkeit als Maßnahmen erklärt werden, die man gezwungen war zu ergreifen. Kaum einer traut sich zu sagen: Es ist mir eine Ehre, alles Menschenmögliche für die Flüchtlinge zu tun. Was diese Erfahrungen bei 55 den Flüchtlingen selbst auslöst, können wir nicht wissen, müsste man abwarten, aber sozialpsychologisch ahnen kann man es schon. Ablehnung und Abwertung in gesellschaftlichen Systemen führt zu einem Gefühl der Ohnmacht. Und diese Ohnmacht 60 ist Sprengstoff für nachfolgende Generationen. Menschen, die am Limit leben, sind sensibel und werden früher oder später spüren, dass sie nicht willkommen sind. (…)

Es ist alles so armselig und hysterisch. Deutsch- 65 land hat es, so zumindest der derzeitige Eindruck, verlernt, was Krieg und Vertreibung mit Menschen anrichtet. Wir haben es verlernt, das Leid der anderen zu unserem Leid zu machen. Diese Denkleistung ist aber die wichtigste Voraussetzung für Solidarität. 70

(482 Wörter)
Mely Kiyak, *Die Zeit*, 2016

Autor: Hartmut Klose, Seevetal
Textquelle: http://www.zeit.de/kultur/2016-02/fluechtlinge-deutschland-kiyaks-deutschstunde, 10.02.2016 (c) ZEIT ONLINE GmbH

A B

A

Interview

1. What do you think of when you hear the term e-waste?

2. What sort of e-waste does your family make?

3. How do you and your family dispose of your e-waste?

4. What can you do to reduce the e-waste in your home?

5. How can the government help to reduce it?

6. In your opinion, is e-waste a global problem? Give some examples to illustrate your opinion.

 Klett
© Ernst Klett Verlag GmbH, Stuttgart 2018.
Alle Rechte vorbehalten. ISBN 978-3-12-834264-1

Monologue Partner A

 Talk about these pictures. What message do they send?

Klett
© Ernst Klett Verlag GmbH, Stuttgart 2018.
Alle Rechte vorbehalten. ISBN 978-3-12-834264-1

Monologue Partner B

👤 *Talk about these pictures. What message do they send?*

Dialogue Partner A

👥 *You are preparing a presentation with your partner on your future in the global village.*
Talk about your respective pictures and choose two of them to illustrate your talk.

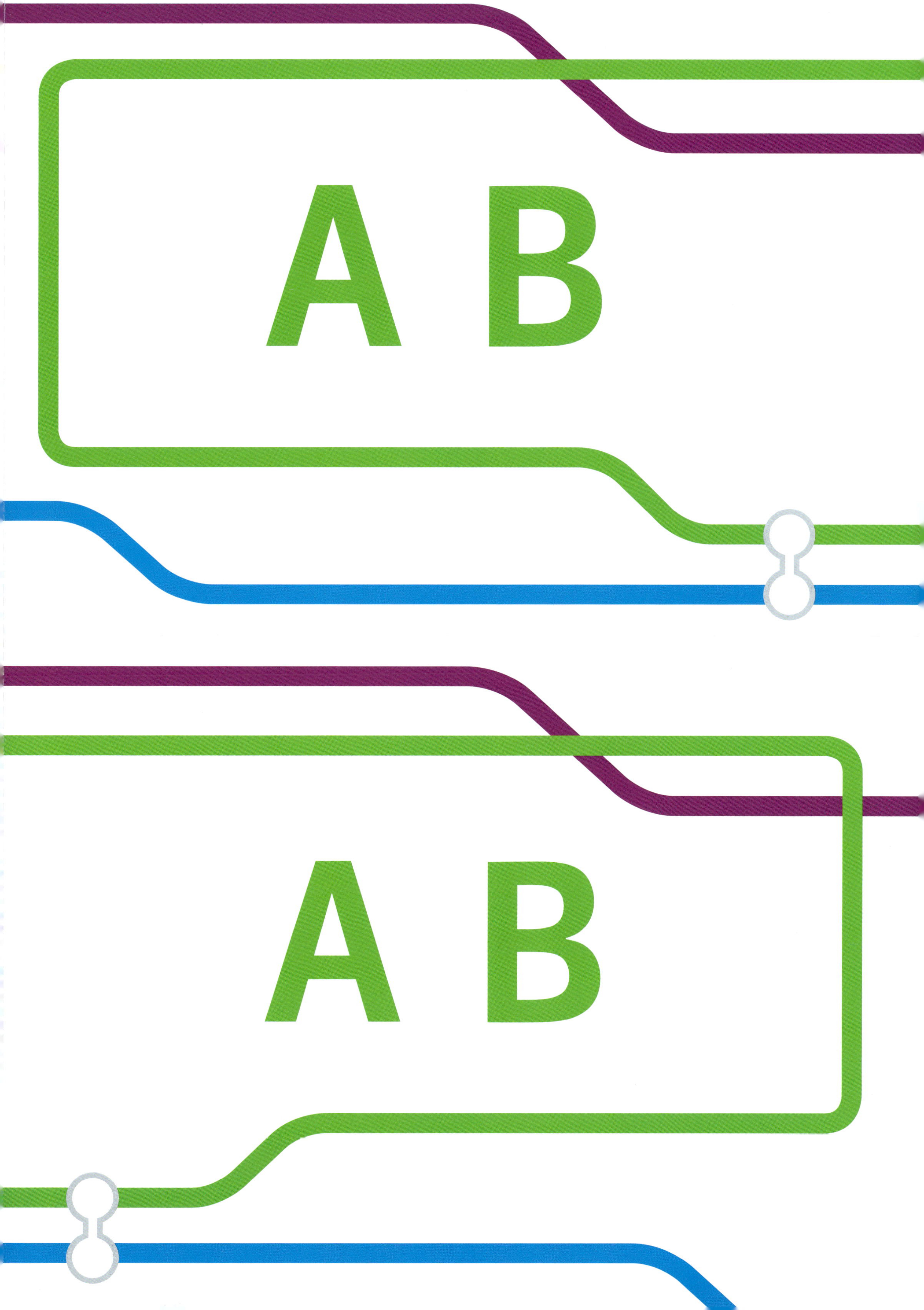
A B
A B

Dialogue Partner B

 *You are preparing a presentation with your partner on your future in the global village. Talk about your respective pictures and choose two of them to illustrate your talk.*

Partner A

 *Describe the picture and talk about the problem it presents.*

 *Your school ECO Club is planning a "Say no to plastic bags" day in your local area. With your partner, discuss possible activities and make three suggestions for an action plan to put forward at your next club meeting.*

Partner B

 *Describe the situation and the atmosphere in the picture.*

 *Your school ECO Club is planning a "Say no to plastic bags" day in your local area. With your partner, discuss possible activities and make three suggestions for an action plan to put forward at your next club meeting.*

Partner A

🧍 *Describe the picture. What problems is the picture trying to illustrate?*

👥 *With your partner, discuss the effectiveness of boycotting garments produced in countries where low pay and working conditions are commonplace. In doing so, consider what else can be done to draw attention to bad working conditions and to improve the situation of workers in such countries.*

Partner B

🧍 *Describe the picture. What problems is the picture trying to illustrate?*

👥 *With your partner, discuss the effectiveness of boycotting garments produced in countries where low pay and working conditions are commonplace. In doing so, consider what else can be done to draw attention to bad working conditions and to improve the situation of workers in such countries.*

Teacher and A/B **Test 4** Crossing borders

Interview

1. **Would you like to study abroad?**	Why? Why not?
2. **What do you think is the best way to get to know a different culture?**	
3. **If you could travel to a country of your choice, where would you like to go, and why?**	
4. **What does the term "culture shock" mean to you?**	
5. **How would you prepare an exchange partner for her/his stay in Germany?**	
6. **'Cross-cultural understanding is more important today than ever before.' Do you agree?**	… and why do you think so?

A B

A B

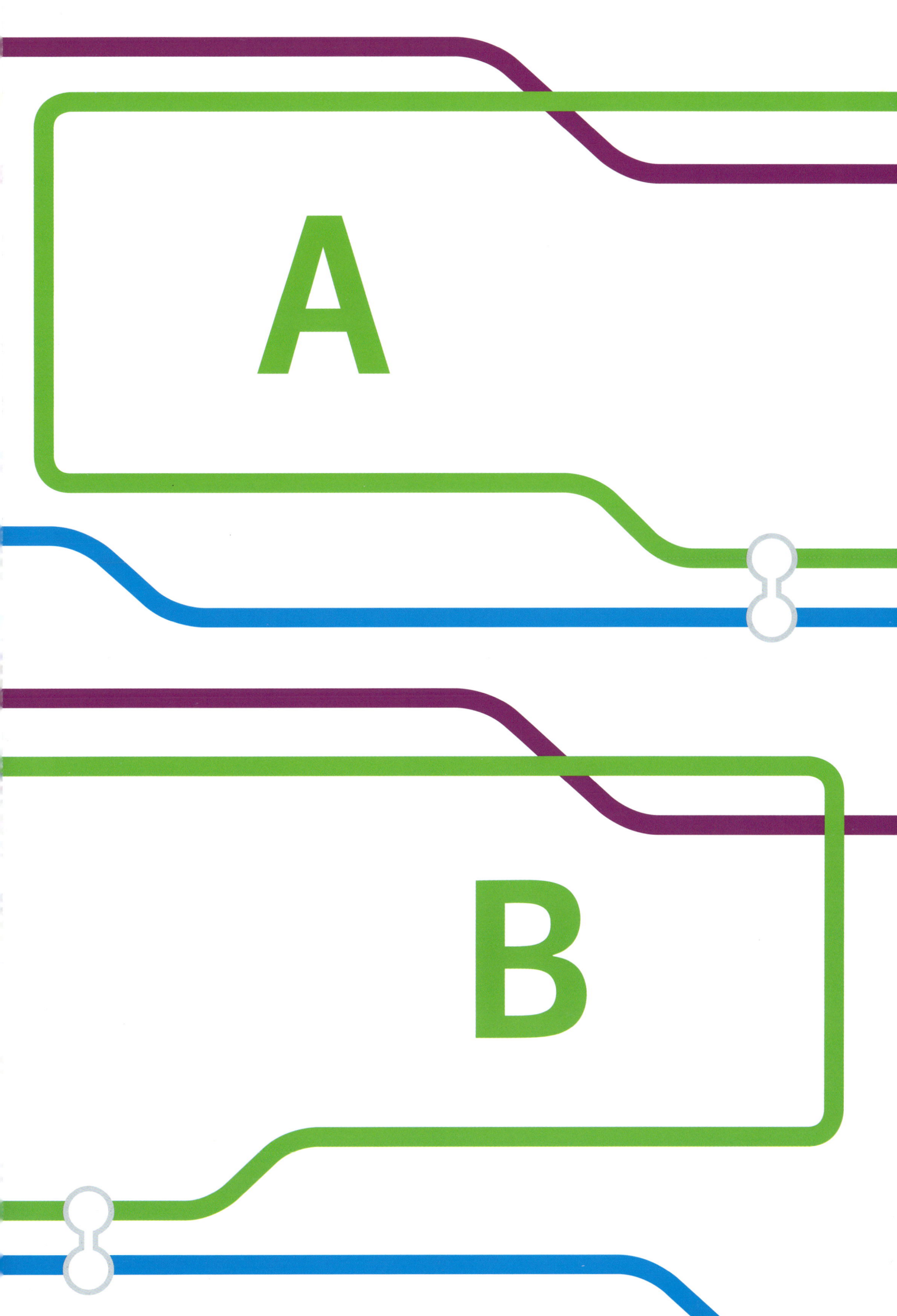

Monologue Partner A

👤 *Talk about these pictures. What message do they send?*

Monologue Partner B

👤 *Talk about these pictures. What message do they send?*

Dialogue Partner A

👥 *You and your partner want to volunteer for a month on a project abroad.*
Discuss the ideas for projects on your cards and whether you have got the motivation and the qualifications
to really help. Try to agree on two of the projects you could apply for.

Child care

Teaching

Feeding the hungry

Animal care

Dialogue Partner B

👥 *You and your partner want to volunteer for a month on a project abroad.*
Discuss the ideas for projects on your cards and whether you have got the motivation and the qualifications
to really help. Try to agree on two of the projects you could apply for.

Conservation and environment

Sports and coaching

Building

Water, sanitation, hygiene

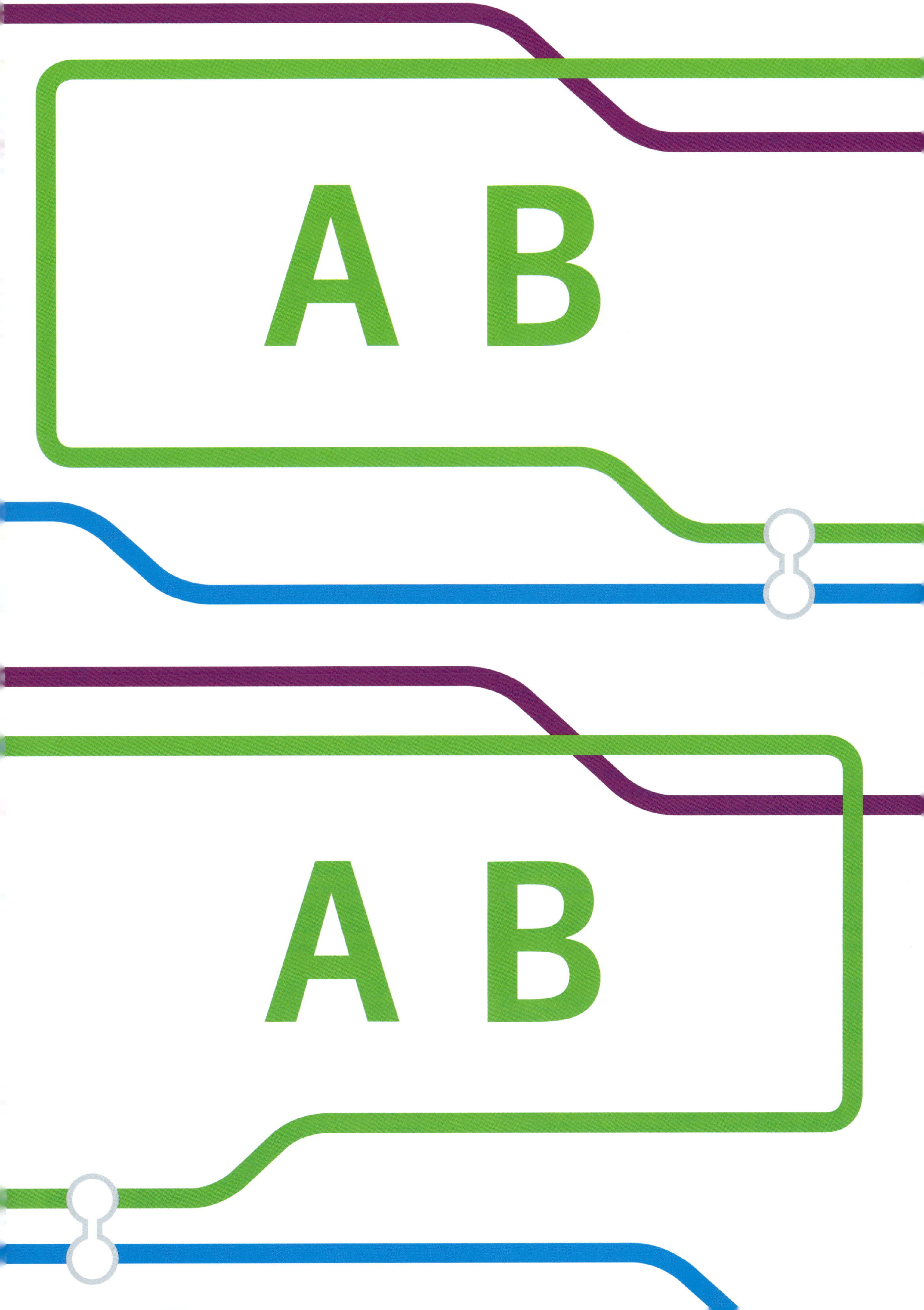
A B
A B

Partner A

👤 *Describe the picture and say what it means to you.*

👥 *You have been asked to write a text on "Crossing borders" for the English department's web page on your school website. With your partner, discuss the pros and cons of travelling and studying abroad before agreeing on three important points you would like to make in your text.*

Partner B

👤 *Describe the picture and say what it means to you.*

👥 *You have been asked to write a text on "Crossing borders" for the English department's web page on your school website. With your partner, discuss the pros and cons of travelling and studying abroad before agreeing on three important points you would like to make in your text.*

Partner A

👤 *Describe the picture. Say what you think of backpacking and whether you would prefer another way of spending time abroad. Give your reasons.*

👥 *One of you has won a photography competition to go on a two-week backpacking trip to [choose a country] with a friend of your choice (your partner). However, you must create a "Welcome to [country's name]" photo report. Discuss where you would like to go and what ideas you already have for your photo report.*

Partner B

👤 *Describe the picture. Say what you think of backpacking and whether you would prefer another way of spending time abroad. Give your reasons.*

👥 *One of you has won a photography competition to go on a two-week backpacking trip to [choose a country] with a friend of your choice (your partner). However, you must create a "Welcome to [country's name]" photo report. Discuss where you would like to go and what ideas you already have for your photo report.*

Partner A

Describe the picture and say whether you would like to travel to this destination. Give your reasons.

You are members of a team working for an advertising company that is making a short film to promote tourism in South Africa. With your partner consider which aspects of South Africa you want to present in your film and the way you want to structure it.

Partner B

Describe the picture and say whether you would like to travel to this destination. Give your reasons.

You are members of a team working for an advertising company that is making a short film to promote tourism in South Africa. With your partner consider which aspects of South Africa you want to present in your film and the way you want to structure it.

Partner A

Describe the picture. Explain what a township is and suggest what life may be like for people living here.

Discuss the pros and cons of participating in a voluntary "Community Service Learning" project in a township while studying in South Africa for a year. You can add other suggestions for a voluntary project.

Partner B

Describe the picture. Explain why you would (not) like to work in a township school in South Africa.

Discuss the pros and cons of participating in a voluntary "Community Service Learning" project in a township while studying in South Africa for a year. You can add other suggestions for a voluntary project.

Course: _____ Date: _____ Name: _____

Writing

Migration to the UK

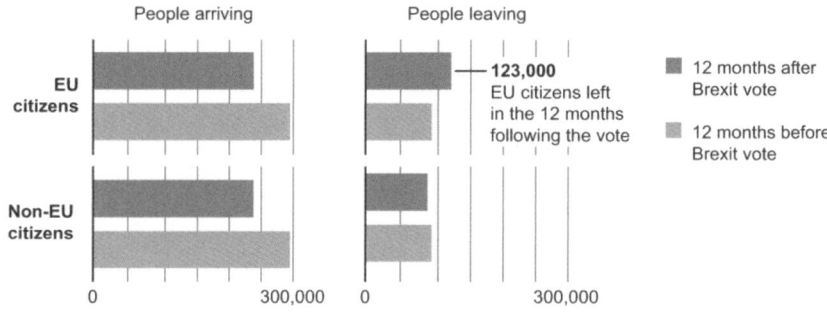

1 *Describe how migration to and from Great Britain changed in the 24 months around the Brexit vote. Refer to the bar chart.*

2 *In light of your findings examine the validity of the message in the cartoon.*

3 *Comment on Prof. Portes' position:*
Professor Jonathan Portes of King's College, London, who works for the research group "UK in a Changing Europe", said the statistics showed the country has become a "less attractive place for European migrants". "Whatever your views on the impact of immigration, it cannot be good news that the UK is a less attractive place to live and work, and that we will be poorer as a result," he said.

Writing

Diversity

1 *Describe the two cartoons.*

2 *Contrast the messages of the cartoons with the ideas that Ndéla Faye presents in the following quotation:*
"I love being able to choose to be whoever I want, wherever I go. My many masks are a storyboard of all that I am. I've gradually built myself an identity that is a collection of pieces, each of which I've handpicked; choosing the best bits in order to create a whole." (Ndéla Faye, The Guardian, 2016)

3 *With reference to the cartoons and the quotation, discuss whether compliance[1] with generally accepted standards of society is a typical problem faced by immigrants.*

1 compliance *here: Zustimmung zu, Annahme von*

Autor: Hartmut Klose, Seevetal
Textquelle: 1. ONS Quarterly Migration Statistics, November 2017; 2. Professor Jonathan Portes © 2017 The Independent; 3. Copyright Guardian News & Media Ltd 2016
Bildquellen: 1. CartoonStock Ltd (Whitworth, James), Bath; 2. toonpool.com (Piero Tonin), Berlin; 3. toonpool.com (Humoresque), Berlin

Course: _____ Date: _____ Name: _____

Reading and writing

Spanish sperm whale death linked to UK supermarket supplier's plastic

Sperm whale on Spanish southern coast had swallowed 17kg of plastic waste dumped by greenhouses supplying produce to the UK.

A dead sperm whale that washed up on Spain's south coast had swallowed 17kg of plastic waste dumped into the sea by farmers tending greenhouses that produce tomatoes and other
5 vegetables for British supermarkets.

Scientists were amazed to find the 4.5 tonne whale had swallowed 59 different bits of plastic – most of it thick transparent sheeting used to build greenhouses in southern Almeria and Granada. A
10 clothes hanger, an ice-cream tub and bits of mattress were also found.

The plastic had eventually blocked the animal's stomach and killed it, according to researchers from the Doñana national park research centre in
15 Andalusia.

Researchers at first found it hard to believe that the 10-metre animal had swallowed the vast amount of plastic they found protruding through a tear in its stomach.
20 In all the whale's stomach contained two dozen pieces of transparent plastic, some plastic bags, nine metres of rope, two stretches of hosepipe, two small flower pots and a plastic spray canister. All were typical of the closely packed Almeria
25 greenhouses that cover about 40,000 hectares – and are clearly visible in satellite photographs taken from space.

Desert-like Almeria has transformed itself into Europe's winter market garden thanks to the plastic
30 greenhouses where plants are grown in beds of perlite stones and drip-fed chemical fertilisers. Local farmers report that Tesco, Waitrose and Sainsbury's are all valued customers.

Estimates of how much plastic waste is generated vary from 45,000 tonnes to more than 35 88,000 tonnes.

Much is treated in special waste centres, but environmentalists complain that local riverbeds are often awash with plastic detritus[1] and, with greenhouses built right up to the high-tide line, some 40 also ends up in the sea.

"The problem of degraded plastics that are no longer recyclable still remains," Renaud de Stephanis, lead researcher at Doñana, and his team reported in the *Marine Pollution Bulletin*. 45 Only about 1,000 sperm whales – the world's biggest toothed whales – are thought to live in the Mediterranean. They live for up to 60 years and are often killed after getting caught in nets or being hit by ships. 50

Now another man-made danger has been detected. "These animals feed in waters near an area completely flooded by the greenhouse industry, making them vulnerable to its waste products if adequate treatment of this industry's debris[2] is not in 55 place," warned de Stephanis.

(415 words)
Giles Tremlett, *The Guardian*, 2013

1 detritus waste ● **2 debris** rubbish

1   COMPREHENSION
Outline the actual reasons why the sperm whale died.

2   ANALYSIS
Explain the connection between ecology and economy in the Almeria region. Refer to the text.

3   EVALUATION
Give a short outline of another environmental issue (What is the problem and why?) and try to find possible solutions to improve the situation.

Course: _____ Date: _____ Name: _____

Reading

1 SHORT ANSWERS
Explain what these numbers refer to:

a) 4.5: _____

b) 9: _____

c) 59: _____

d) 60: _____

e) 40,000: _____

2 TRUE OR FALSE?
Tick true or false. Give the line numbers and the first and last three words of the quote to support your choice.

	TRUE	FALSE
1. A sperm whale had dumped 17kg of plastic waste. l./ll.: _____		
2. Only plastic farming equipment was found in the whale. l./ll.: _____		
3. In the whale's stomach, there were 24 pieces of transparent plastic. l./ll.: _____		
4. The plastic waste is visible from space. l./ll.: _____		
5. In this region of Southern Spain there isn't much rain. l./ll.: _____		
6. The products of that region are also exported to UK supermarkets. l./ll.: _____		
7. Only a small part of the plastic waste ends up in the rivers. l./ll.: _____		
8. Some plastic ends up in the sea because the greenhouses were built too close to the coast. l./ll.: _____		
9. Sperm whales are rare. l./ll.: _____		
10. Sperm whales are often killed by fishermen because whale meat is expensive. l./ll.: _____		
11. The author makes an appeal to the consumers' sense of responsibility. l./ll.: _____		
12. The author lists examples to visualise the dangers for the animals. l./ll.: _____		

Autor: Matthias Bode, Marburg

Course: _____ **Date:** _____ **Name:** _____

Reading and writing

The following diary entries covering the events in summer directly follow the excerpts from The Carbon Diaries *in your English book:*

The Carbon Diaries **by Saci Lloyd**

Mon, June 1st
No rain for weeks and weeks. Dad tried to hand out a load of new house rules at dinner today. He wants us to shower in a bucket for 1 minute max and then
5 throw the water on the garden. No more dishwasher, no more washing machine, one clothes wash per person per week, by hand. The toilet rule's the most disgusting part: basically – if it's yellow let it mellow, if it's brown flush it down. Dad tried to make a joke
10 out of it. I saw Mum give him this look like she wondered how she'd ever fancied him. She went over to the cooker.

Fri, June 26th
The Mayor's given in to Thames Water. He's forcing
15 a compulsory water-rationing system on us. Effective immediately. Basically everyone's got to get a water meter fitted in the next 3 weeks. Government vans will deliver them street by street across the city and then we've got to put them in ourselves. The limit's
20 going to be 90 litres per person per day. That's a cut of 60 litres. Go over and the taps run dry.

Wed, July 1st
I don't believe it. Without asking Mum, Dad has traded her car for a wheelbarrow full of tools, 5 hens,
25 a cockerel, a scooter, a pig and a sty! He's like a village idiot.

Mum came back from work and stared, dumb, at the empty spot where the Saab used to be parked. Then she went upstairs and started to throw clothes into a suitcase. I followed her and leaned against the   30
doorway. 'Where are you going?' 'Away from that man,' she ground out between clenched teeth.

Thurs, Aug 6th
It reached 43°C in Birmingham today. The hottest ever recorded temperature in the UK. Our water   35
goes tomorrow. Only hospitals and vital industry's going to stay connected. Not that you'd want to go to hospital, they're all packed out. Queen Elizabeth's Hospital's got a tent set up in the car park to deal with all the people collapsing in the heat.   40

Fri, Aug 7th
Totally forgot. Went to the bathroom this morning and no water in the taps. Had to spit out my toothpaste and clean my teeth off with a towel.

Mon, Aug 10th   45
Man, it's like a police state. There's a 24-hour patrol all over the city – and a hotline for grassing up your neighbours. It's prison for stealing water – what happened to drugs and mugging?

(414 words)
From: *The Carbon Diaries* by Saci Lloyd

1   COMPREHENSION
Outline the events of that summer.

2   ANALYSIS
Compare the consequences of water rationing in this passage to energy rationing as described in the passage in your English book.

3   EVALUATION
The German edition of The Carbon Diaries *(2008) is called* Euer schönes Leben kotzt mich an: Ein Umweltroman aus dem Jahr 2015: *Discuss whether this is a good title.*

Autor: Matthias Bode, Marburg
Textquelle: from: The Carbon Diaries, Saci Lloyd, Hodder Children's Books, London, 2008

Course: _____ Date: _____ Name: _____

Reading

SENTENCE COMPLETION

Complete the sentences with the information from the text.

1. It is a very dry summer because _____

   _____

2. The family should flush the toilet when _____

   _____

3. It's obvious that Dad is funny when _____

   _____

4. Thames Water is _____

   _____

5. Government representatives will _____

6. The daily pre-crisis water consumption was _____

7. You can see that Dad wants to produce eggs locally when _____

   _____

8. Mum wants to leave Dad because _____

9. Companies producing luxury products do not _____

   _____

10. Many people suffer from the heat as _____

    _____

11. A police state is established because _____

    _____

12. The installation of water meters does not solve the water crisis because _____

    _____

13. The reader learns that the narrator opposes the new rules when _____

    _____

14. The author creates a tense atmosphere by _____

    _____

15. Living conditions for the family become harder because _____

    _____

Autor: Matthias Bode, Marburg

Course: _____ **Date:** _____ **Name:** _____

Listening

◎ **How German wood detectives protect endangered species**

SENTENCE COMPLETION
Complete the sentences.

1. Tigers and pandas are examples _____

2. The Thünen Institute is located _____

3. In the beginning the speaker wants to _____ the scientist.

4. The scientist needed a few seconds to identify the _____ of tree species.

5. The identification of the species takes _____

6. Ebony is _____

7. Half of all Amazon _____ are in danger of extinction.

8. The guitar came from _____

9. The tested fence posts were made of _____

Second listening: Complete the sentences.

10. Koch has about _____ wood samples.

11. CITES was established in _____

12. Trees are protected by law in _____ countries.

13. Gerald Koch found _____ different types of timber in one guitar.

14. CITES is _____

    _____

15. Andrea Olbrich can identify species by looking at _____

Course: _____ Date: _____ Name: _____

Listening

 Fishy Business in Vietnam

SENTENCE COMPLETION
Complete the sentences.

1. The fish industry is _____

2. Annual seafood exports total about _____ dollars.

3. The exports go to _____

4. Pangasius farming is _____

5. Evidence of factory farming includes _____
    _____

6. The difference between advertising and reality is _____ because ads
    _____

7. Higher standards are demanded by _____
    _____

8. The power of the consumer will become clear if _____
    _____

9. In China, on the other hand, _____
    _____

10. There are no water treatment plants so _____
    _____

11. Seafood farms are important for Vietnam because _____
    _____

12. The conflict between ecology and economy in Vietnam is whether _____
    _____

13. The author of this report is critical of factory farming as you can see _____
    _____

Mediation

In your Erasmus project "Think globally, act locally", schools from all over Europe are working together on environmental issues. You decide to write an email to your partner schools informing them of
- *the relevant facts about paper coffee cups in Germany;*
- *the discussion in Germany;*
- *the author's attitude regarding this issue.*

Die große Heuchelei um den Mehrweg-Kaffeebecher

Der Mehrwegkaffeebecher ist in den letzten Monaten zum neuen Star der Umweltbewegten aufgestiegen. Wer den Muntermacher aus Einwegbehältnissen schlürft, stellt sich dagegen
5　automatisch auf eine Stufe mit Dieselfahrern, Rauchern und Plastiktütenträgern. Auf Partys zu behaupten, dass es wichtigere Probleme auf der Welt gebe, kommt einer Aufforderung zum Rausschmiss gleich.
10　Es gibt ein sicheres Zeichen dafür, dass der Mehrwegbecher in der Mitte der Konsumgesellschaft angekommen ist: Große Konzerne und ganze Städte machen mit bei der Bewegung. [...] Ganze Städte springen auf den Zug auf. München will Pächtern
15　städtischer Kaffeeausgaben Einweglösungen noch vor dem Herbst verbieten. Im Stadtrat fiel der Beschluss ohne Gegenstimmen. Rosenheim versucht es mit einem Pfandsystem, Freiburg mit dem „Freiburg Cup". Dutzende Cafés, Bäckereien
20　und Eisdielen beteiligen sich bereits, meldet die Stadtverwaltung stolz. [...]
　　Tatsächlich eignen sich die Ex-und-hopp-Becher ideal als Kampagnenobjekt und Symbolgegenstand für ein gutes Umweltgewissen. Dafür gibt es
25　mehrere Gründe. Erstens: Das Thema Kaffee interessiert alle. Jeder Deutsche trinkt im Schnitt jährlich 162 Liter, mehr als von jedem anderen Getränk. Zweitens: Das Hassobjekt Pappbecher ist augenfällig, man wird immer wieder daran erinnert.
30　In Parkanlagen, auf Autobahnrandstreifen oder zwischen Bahngeleisen rotten die achtlos weggeworfenen Exemplare quälend langsam vor sich hin und bieten idealen Unterschlupf für allerlei Ungeziefer – Müll übelster Sorte. Drittens: Es kostet
35　den Einzelnen nicht viel, sich von den Umweltsündern abzusetzen. Bei Home-Discountern gibt es Thermokaffeebecher zur Dauernutzung mit Griff, Deckel und 350 Milliliter Fassungsvermögen schon ab zwei Euro [...]

Folgt man Umweltverbänden, ist es höchste Zeit, 40 sich dem Thema zu widmen. [...] 31.000 Tonnen Abfall kämen so alljährlich zusammen, plus 9000 Tonnen durch die unvermeidlichen Plastikdeckelchen, die das Heißgetränk bei der Stadtwanderung am Überschwappen hindern sollen. 45 Erschreckende Zahlen. Aber [...] [g]emessen an den rund 46 Millionen Tonnen haushaltstypischen Siedlungsabfällen, die laut Statistischem Bundesamt jährlich anfallen, machen die Kaffeebehältnisse weniger als ein Promille aus. Anders ausgedrückt: Je 50 Kilo Hausmüll entfallen nur 0,9 Gramm auf Einwegbecher.

Den Boom der Mitbringbehälter beobachten viele Hygienefachleute zudem mit Argwohn. [...] Auch der Deutsche Kaffeeverband ist skeptisch. Die 55 mitgebrachten Behältnisse könnten in nichtsterilen Handtaschen oder Rucksäcken mit Bakterien in Berührung gekommen sein, es sei „ein Anfassen mit nicht gereinigten Händen" denkbar, womöglich klebten Rückstände an Deckeln oder Bechern. [...] 60 Ein weiterer Einwand dürfte den Mehrwegbecherhelden allerdings noch weniger schmecken als die Hygienebedenken: Es ist durchaus unsicher, ob Mehrwegbecher nach Abwägung aller Aspekte überhaupt besser für die 65 Umwelt sind. Schließlich müssen mehrfach benutzte Becher, egal ob aus Kunststoff, Edelstahl oder Keramik, energieintensiv gespült werden. Ihre Herstellung setzt Klimagas frei, der Transport belastet die Umwelt. [...] 70

Am Ende bleibt ein Disziplinproblem – das gedankenlose Wegschmeißen. Bis zu 17 Prozent des auf den Straßen und Grünflächen herumliegenden Mülls seien Einwegbecher, so die Düsseldorfer Verbraucherzentrale. Das ist nicht nur 75 hässlich, sondern auch teuer. Allein die Uni Tübingen gab 2015 rund 16.000 Euro fürs Einsammeln von Pappbechern aus.

(460 Wörter)
Michael Gassmann, *Welt.de*, 2017

Course: _____ Date: _____ Name: _____

Writing

Writing a blog post

"Just what you asked for...made in the US by adult US citizens...that will be $1,795.00."

Your online magazine "For a better world" is covering the topic of fair trade this week. Present the situation shown in the cartoon.

Explain the dilemma the consumer is facing here. Refer to material dealt with in class.

End your blog post with references to "fair" products and state your opinion on the consumer's dilemma.

Write about 300 words.

Writing

Writing a speech

Write a speech to convince fellow teenagers to recycle their old mobile phones. Refer to material dealt with in class as well as to the infographic at hand. Write about 300 words.

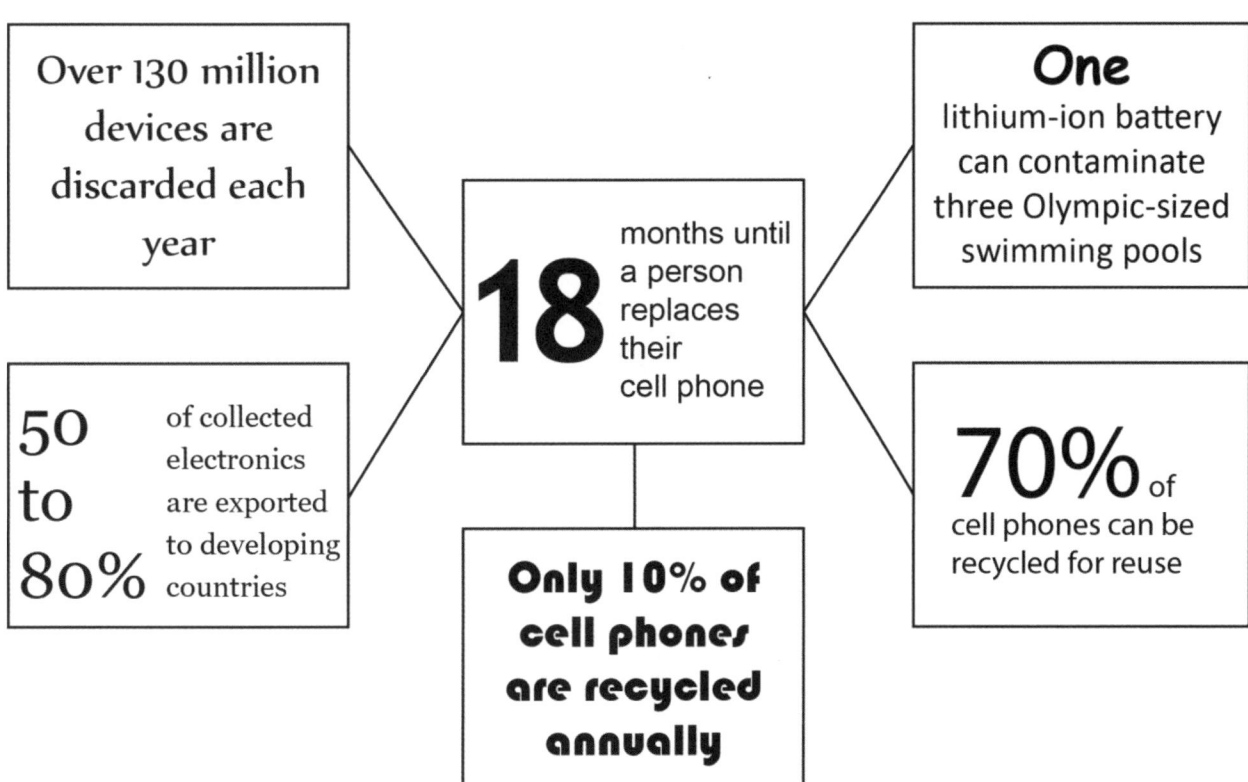

Cell phone recycling by the numbers

Autor: Matthias Bode, Marburg
Textquelle: www.e-Cycle.com, 2017
Bildquelle:www.CartoonStock.com (Delgado, Roy), Bath

Course: _____   Date: _____   Name: _____

Reading and writing

Nicky Gordon, a British student, reports on her year abroad in Germany.

Learning the local language made my year abroad unforgettable

Understanding German opened up a new world of under-the-radar flea markets and student nights.

When I started a degree in English language and literature, I hadn't intended to study abroad, let alone[1] start learning German. But having recently returned from my year abroad in Germany, I can say 5 that making the effort to learn the language really enhanced my Erasmus[2] experience.

With language translation technology advancing all the time, it's tempting to rely on Google Translate and smartphone apps as an alternative to language 10 learning. But a second language shouldn't be an optional luxury. Researchers have discovered that intensive language learning can increase the size of your brain in as little as three months. (…)

From my own experience, learning the language 15 lets you travel beyond the well-known tourist trails, gain an authentic student experience and expand your social network beyond the international clan. The process of learning German on my Erasmus year was a stark contrast to my pre-departure 20 language course at university, where bleary-eyed students sat passively and stumbled through oral exercises.

Instead, language learning abroad was dynamic and part of my lifestyle – from chatting with sales 25 assistants to preparing presentations with course mates. It meant being part of the local community. Visiting language exchange cafés – where international and German students meet up to improve their European language of choice – was a 30 great way to practice in a relaxed space and meet a diverse range of people.

Not being afraid to make mistakes is crucial to learning a language. By abandoning that comfortable phrase "Ich spreche nur ein bisschen Deutsch!" (I speak only a little German), I made progress and it 35 was appreciated by friends and locals alike. Having a tandem partner[3] helped my conversational German and I learned to avoid common pitfalls such as mistaking "Mir ist heiß" for "Ich bin heiß" . Both phrases mean "I am hot", but "Ich bin heiß" suggests 40 that you think you're hot as in sexy!

Aside from avoiding social embarrassment, by getting to know German students I discovered under-the-radar flea markets and student nights, learned how to cook authentic German dishes and gained in- 45 the-know[4] travel buddies. […] I enjoyed local street parades during public holidays like Fastnacht, and indulged fully in the coffee and cake culture.

Even when it comes to eating out, knowing the language works to your advantage. In more than a 50 few traditional German restaurants, the English menus didn't contain all the dishes listed on the German menu.

Learning the language has saved me from getting on the wrong train, after last-minute platform 55 changes were announced in German. It's also an impressive asset when friends and family come to visit, giving them extra reassurance that you're able to survive independently.

So why not learn the local language on your 60 Erasmus year abroad? It'll improve your employability, while letting you take part fully in local life.

(494 words)
Nicky Gordon, *The Guardian*, 2014

1 let alone *ganz zu schweigen von* ● **2 Erasmus** European student exchange programme ● **3 tandem partner** partner who speaks the native language and wants to learn your language ● **4 in-the-know** being well-informed

1   COMPREHENSION
Explain why, according to Nicky Gordon, learning the local language is so essential for students who spend a year abroad.

2   ANALYSIS
Analyse how Nicky Gordon tries to make the text convincing and interesting.

3   EVALUATION
You were Nicky's tandem partner during her year in Germany. After her return to the UK, you write her an email in which you talk about the good times you had and in which you thank her.

Autor: Reiner Verspai, Rheinbach
Textquelle: Copyright Guardian News & Media Ltd 2014

Course: _____   **Date:** _____   **Name:** _____

Reading

SENTENCE COMPLETION
Read the text and then complete the following sentences.

1. Nicky Gordon was not really interested in learning German before _____

   _____

2. Gordon thinks that language learning is extremely important for people today although modern technology _

   _____

3. Gordon refers to scientific proof for the importance of language learning when she says that_____

   _____

4. Gordon points out that if you do not learn the language, most of the new friends you make_____

   _____

5. The terms "bleary-eyed" and "stumbled" (ll. 20/21) suggest that, according to Gordon, in language courses

   at university students _____

   _____

6. In Germany Gordon stopped saying "Ich spreche nur ein bisschen Deutsch!" because_____

   _____

   _____

7. Gordon avoided some common misunderstandings of German expressions only thanks to _____

   _____

8. German students helped Gordon to discover "under-the-radar" flea markets, which means that _____

   _____

9. Knowing the German language also helped her with food and eating out because (*three items*)_____

   _____

   _____

   _____

10. According to Gordon it can be important for your job life to speak a foreign language because it makes

    _____

11. The end of the text makes it clear that it is Gordon's main intention_____

    _____

Course: _____ Date: _____ Name: _____

Reading and writing

Excerpt from *Are you experienced?* by W. Sutcliffe

W. Sutcliffe's novel Are you experienced? *is about the experiences of Liz and Dave, two young people from Britain on their first visit to India. Having arrived at Delhi airport, the two are about to get into a bus to take them to their hostel. An assistant has just put Dave's bags on top of the bus. Dave is the narrator of the story.*

When he came back down, he started doing a strange upward nodding gesture and saying 'munee - munee'.

'He wants money,' said Liz.

5 'Why should I give him money? It's his job. I was quite willing to put it up there myself.'

'Just give him some money, for God's sake. I'll get in and grab some seats.'

'I haven't got any money yet, have I? It doesn't
10 exactly look like he takes traveller's cheques.'

'Just give him anything.'

'Like what? A roll of loo paper? Yesterday's Guardian[1]?' She ignored me and got on the bus.

'Munee. Munee.'

15 'I haven't got any.'

'Munee.'

He was beginning to tug at my clothes now, and the crowd of onlookers was closing in –

'Look, mate – I haven't got any money yet. I
20 have to go to a bank.'

'MUNEE!'

I turned out my pockets to show him that I didn't have any money, and out fell a whole load of English coins. He gave me an evil stare, then bent over to
25 pick up the coins. There was a mini riot while several people scrabbled for the cash, so I sneaked away and got into the bus, hoping that I'd be out of sight before they realized that it was only English money.

During the bag episode all the seats had gone,
30 and Liz was standing somewhere near the back. I went and joined her.

'Just in time,' I said.

Half an hour later, with the bus jammed full of people, the driver started revving the engine.

Half an hour after that, with the bus containing 35 twice as many people as it had when I'd thought it was full, and with the man in the red turban still shouting at me through the window, we crawled out of the airport.

'This is awful,' I said. 40

'What's awful?' said Liz.

'This. Everything.'

'What did you expect?' she said, with an unforgiving glare.

'Is this what it's meant to be like?' 45

'I suppose so.'

'This is what we've come for?'

'Yes. It's India.'

'Jesus. I don't believe this.'

I suddenly felt as if my stomach had been filled 50 with pebbles. This was all wrong. I'd come to the wrong place. I hadn't even eaten anything yet, and I felt sick already — from the heat, the crowds, the claustrophobia[2] — and pure blind fear.

What the hell had I done? Why had I come to 55 this awful country? I was going to hate it. I already knew. There was no way I could possibly get used to any of this. And now I was stuck here.

This was bad. This was very bad.

(435 words)

From: William Sutcliffe, *Are you experienced?*, 1999

---

1 Guardian British newspaper ● **2 claustrophobia** fear of places with no way of escape

1   COMPREHENSION
Summarise what happens at the bus station.

2   ANALYSIS
Explain how Dave feels during these first few moments in India and analyse how the author expresses Dave's feelings in this extract.

3   EVALUATION
It is very important for tourists to be well-informed about the country they travel to. Do you agree?
Write a comment and refer to Dave's experiences in this scene.

Autor: Reiner Verspai, Rheinbach
Textquelle: From: Are you experienced?, © W. Sutcliff 1997, Hamish Hamilton, London

Course: _____   Date: _____   Name: _____

Reading

MULTIPLE CHOICE

Read the text, then tick the correct answer. Only one answer is correct.

1. At first Dave does not understand what the assistant wants from him because the assistant
   - ☐ a) does not speak English.
   - ☐ b) does not speak loud enough.
   - ☐ c) does not pronounce his words correctly.
   - ☐ d) makes a strange gesture.

2. When the assistant asks for money
   - ☐ a) Liz leaves Dave alone.
   - ☐ b) Liz talks to him.
   - ☐ c) Liz offers to give him some.
   - ☐ d) Liz does not understand him either.

3. Dave does not want to give the assistant money
   - ☐ a) because he has only got coins.
   - ☐ b) because he thinks the assistant is paid for the job.
   - ☐ c) because he spent his money buying *The Guardian*.
   - ☐ d) because he thinks the assistant is very unfriendly.

4. When Dave shows the assistant the inside of his pockets and some coins fall out
   - ☐ a) there is a small riot because people are angry at Dave.
   - ☐ b) many other people try to get hold of some money.
   - ☐ c) Dave gives the assistant some coins.
   - ☐ d) the assistant is finally happy.

5. When Dave gets on the bus
   - ☐ a) Liz is waiting for him.
   - ☐ b) the assistant follows him.
   - ☐ c) he sits down next to Liz.
   - ☐ d) the driver starts the engine.

6. The bus does not leave at once because
   - ☐ a) there is a traffic jam.
   - ☐ b) there are technical problems.
   - ☐ c) Dave is still quarrelling with the assistant.
   - ☐ d) passengers are still boarding the bus.

7. What the "bag episode" shows about Dave is that
   - ☐ a) he is a relaxed type of person.
   - ☐ b) he feels superior to the assistant.
   - ☐ c) he is a generous person.
   - ☐ d) he is an experienced traveller.

8. In this "bag episode" Dave's friend Liz
   - ☐ a) is angry at the assistant.
   - ☐ b) is critical of Dave's behaviour.
   - ☐ c) is totally indifferent.
   - ☐ d) is very patient.

9. What Dave dislikes about India
   - ☐ a) is the great number of people.
   - ☐ b) is the noise.
   - ☐ c) is the fact that things are expensive.
   - ☐ d) is the poverty.

10. Dave's negative feelings about India are reflected in
   - ☐ a) the symbols he uses.
   - ☐ b) the questions he asks.
   - ☐ c) a number of contrasts.
   - ☐ d) a number of exact descriptions.

11. This scene shows that Dave and Liz
   - ☐ a) have both prepared for their stay.
   - ☐ b) both experience a kind of culture shock.
   - ☐ c) have different ideas about their visit.
   - ☐ d) have been a couple for a long time.

Autor: Reiner Verspai, Rheinbach

Course: _____ Date: _____ Name: _____

Listening

◎ **Syrian refugees**

TABLE COMPLETION

Listen to a programme (from 2017) about Syrian refugees in Germany and then complete the following table by answering the questions in words or short sentences. You will hear the recording twice. After each time, you will have three minutes to complete the task. Now you have two minutes to read the questions.

1. Why is Amy (the reporter) waiting at the airport?	_____
2. How many of the refugees from Syria came to Germany in 2015?	_____
3. Where did Amy first meet Mohamed in 2015?	_____
4. What is Mohamed's age?	_____
5. What country did their boat trip start from and where did it take them?	_____
6. How long did they stay in the water on the first trip?	_____
7. Why was the third trip dangerous?	_____
8. What did Nur do before leaving Syria?	_____
9. What is Nur's dream?	_____
10. Apart from learning the language, what made life in Germany difficult in the beginning?	_____
11. What is Nur's greatest worry?	_____
12. Why is Nur glad when she is with other people?	_____
13. Which relatives did Mohamed leave behind?	_____

Course: _____   Date: _____   Name: _____

Listening

⊚ **The five phases of culture shock**

SEQUENCING

Listen to the award-winning podcast 'absolutely intercultural' by Dr. Elmar-Laurent Borgmann, senior lecturer at RheinAhrCampus of Hochschule Koblenz. Every month a new episode is released on various intercultural issues addressed to students. You can listen to more than 200 episodes at www.absolutely-intercultural.com. In this episode, the author talks about the 5 phases of culture shock. Listen to it and then match the phases (1–5) and their characteristics by putting down the correct number in the boxes on the left. You will hear the talk twice. After each time, you will have three minutes to complete the task. Note that there are 3 characteristics that do not fit any of the phases.

Phases of culture shock:
1 = honeymoon period
2 = frustration or negotiation phase
3 = adjustment phase
4 = mastery or acceptance stage
5 = re-entry shock

Phase number	Characteristic of phase
	you start having deeper conversations
	people do not realize you are not from the country
	people show great interest in you
	you do not contact people in your home country as much as before
	concrete problems cause difficulties
	some people do not recognize you any more
	you prefer the new country to your own
	real integration has been achieved
	you start dreaming in the foreign language
	you start to experiment and try things out
	people are not as fascinated by you any more
	you annoy people by talking too much about your experiences
	a feeling of loneliness comes up
	people do not understand what you are saying
	you start to understand more deeply how the country works

Course: _____ Date: _____ Name: _____

Mediation

Projects abroad

Together with an American friend you would like to do a volunteering project in a developing country in the month of April. You have found the following advert by Projects Abroad *online and are interested in the offer. As your friend does not speak German, you inform him about the project and talk about it with him on the phone. Write their dialogue.*

Freiwilligenarbeit: Sozialarbeit in Madagaskar

- Projekt – Standort: Andasibe
- Unterbringung: Gastfamilien
- Preise: ab 1,865 €
- Projektdauer: ab zwei Wochen
5 - Starttermin: Flexibles Startdatum

In unserem Sozialarbeits – Projekt in Madagaskar kannst du dich ehrenamtlich für benachteiligte Kinder einsetzen. Egal, ob du gerade eine Auszeit vom Job suchst, ein Sabbatjahr planst oder noch zur Schule gehst, in diesem Projekt kannst du dich für andere Menschen engagieren und wirst dafür mit der Gastfreundschaft und Herzlichkeit des Landes und seiner Bewohner belohnt werden.

10 **Deine Rolle im Sozialarbeits – Projekt in Madagaskar**

Als Freiwillige/r wirst du im Early Childhood Development Centre in Andasibe eingesetzt, einer Betreuungseinrichtung speziell ausgelegt auf frühkindliche Förderung, wo du dich um Kinder im Alter zwischen 2 und 6 Jahren kümmern wirst. Viele der Kinder kommen aus ärmeren Familien, die sich keinen Kindergartenplatz oder eine Vorschule für ihre Kleinen leisten können. Das Zentrum wird vollständig von
15 Projects Abroad geführt und ist darum das ganze Jahr über auf die Hilfe von Freiwilligen angewiesen. Pädagogisches Ziel des Zentrums ist die Vorbereitung der Kinder auf ihre Schulausbildung. Viele Kinder in Andasibe bringen bei ihrer Einschulung ein sehr geringes Vorwissen über das Alphabet und Zahlen mit und tun sich schwer mit dem Stoff der ersten Klasse. Hier arbeiten wir deshalb mit unseren Freiwilligen daran, sich mit den Kindern spielerisch mit Fibeln, Lesekarten, Zahlenspielen und Sprachstunden in Englisch und
20 Französisch an den Schulstoff heranzutasten. Unsere genauen Projektziele kannst du auch im Madagaskar Care Management Plan nachlesen.
Als Teil deiner Freiwilligenarbeit wirst du den Kindern außerdem Grundlagen der Alltagshygiene näherbringen. Deine Ideen für andere Lernaktivitäten, Sport- und Kunststunden sind herzlich willkommen, um die Kinder für verschiedene Freizeitaktivitäten zu begeistern. Auf diese Weise kannst du den Kindern auf
25 spielerische Art dabei helfen, Talente und Stärken zu entwickeln und auszubauen.
Soziales Engagement, Einfühlungsvermögen und Spaß an der Arbeit sind die wichtigsten Eigenschaften, die du als Freiwillige/r mitbringen solltest. Projects Abroad unterstützt dich während deines gesamten Einsatzes. Wir helfen dir dabei, notwendige Materialien zu beschaffen oder organisieren Aktionstage mit anderen Freiwilligen, bei denen ihr gemeinsam lokale Einrichtungen renoviert oder verschönert.

30 **Freiwilligenarbeit im Juli bis September**

Bitte beachte, dass deine Aufgaben als Freiwillige/r während der großen Schulferien in den Monaten Juli bis September vom normalen Schuljahr abweichen. In dieser Zeit hilfst du, ein Sommercamp für Kinder zwischen 6 und 11 Jahren auf die Beine zu stellen, damit sie in ihren Ferien beschäftigt bleiben. Natürlich dürfen auch die jüngeren Kids an dem Sommerlager teilnehmen. In diesem Fall führst du auch die speziell ausgerichteten
35 Unterrichtsstunden für frühkindliche Förderung weiter. (…)

(412 Wörter)
Projects Abroad-Webseite, 2017

Course: _____   **Date:** _____   **Name:** _____

Writing

Comment on cultural differences

> "Variety is the spice of life."
> (saying)

Explain the metaphor in the quotation and then write a comment on it. In your text, refer to the picture above and to the work done in class ("Crossing borders").

Writing

A blog entry about tourism and travel

> "Travel ought to combine amusement with instruction; but most travellers are so much amused that they refuse to be instructed."
> (Quote by G.K. Chesterton)

While travelling through different countries on your summer holiday, you have often been annoyed at the way many tourists behave. Write a blog entry for your school website on the way tourists often behave and on how they should behave. In your text, refer to the cartoon and the quotation.

Autor: Reiner Verspai, Rheinbach
Textquelle: Quotation from G. K. Chesterton † 1936
Bildquellen: 1. www.CartoonStock.com (Kutal, Firuz), Bath; 2. toonpool.com (Huse), Berlin

Course: _____　Date: _____　Name: _____

Reading and writing

Education

One of the most important areas of concern in South Africa is education. Without an educated population, a country cannot progress not only in terms of economic development but also because of political
5　development. In South Africa, just like in other parts of the world, parents have a strong desire to see their children progress and have a good life; hence, families are willing to make sacrifices for education. Unfortunately, the government has not been able to
10　supply enough classroom spaces for those of school age and many existing government facilities in low-income areas offer poor-quality education.

　　Part of the problem is tied to budget constraints, but there are also administrative and corruption
15　issues. Corruption Watch, a non-government organization, said that between 2012 and 2015 it received more than 1,000 reports of school principals who had stolen cash from school bank accounts.[1] It also reported school principal posts are so lucrative
20　they are bought and sold.

　　As a result of these problems, a thriving private-school market has emerged in South Africa. One private-school firm we visited had more than 100 schools and was expanding rapidly, with more new
25　schools opening each year. Given capacity and quality issues in government schools, as well as a lack of schools in newly developing areas, middle-class families are seeking to enroll their children in lower-cost private schools in greater numbers.
30　The school personnel we spoke with said even poor parents would sacrifice a substantial portion of their income to send their children to these schools, in an attempt to get them the best education possible. Some of the families lived in wood and corrugated
35　steel shacks with no running water or inside toilets.

1 Source: Corruption Watch, "Loss of Principle," October 2015.

The firm's management has been working on a "plug-and-play" model where schools can be established all over the country with a centralized head office that manages information technology, curriculum materials, site locations and overall management.　40

　　Also looking at the government schools, I learned the range of quality varies greatly. Driving through one of the high- income neighborhoods of Cape Town, I saw a beautiful school with excellent buildings and all kinds of sport facilities. I learned students attending　45 that school scored among the highest in academic standards in the country.

　　However, other government schools have overcrowding and very low standards. A school's local governing body can charge additional fees to　50 students to maintain certain standards, facilities, etc., which means the quality of education is better in wealthier neighborhoods, where families can afford high fees, than in poor neighborhoods where families can't.　55

　　At government schools, teacher quality and training is seen as a problem, and apparently, it's not uncommon to find teachers with only a 10th-grade education themselves teaching students in grade 12. This is a legacy of the so-called "bantu" education　60 system during apartheid years, which neglected teacher training for the black population. With the tremendous influence that education has on unemployment and economic advancement, we hope that this area sees some progress so even　65 underprivileged children have access to a good education.

(503 words)
Mark Mobius, 2018

1　COMPREHENSION
Outline the problems in South African education as described in the text.

2　ANALYSIS
Examine the line of arguments and the language the author uses to get his message across.

3　EVALUATION
a)　*Comment on this statement: A good education is necessary to end social inequality in South Africa.*

OR

b)　*You want to improve the educational system in South Africa. Write a letter to the Department of Education explaining what changes are necessary to give underprivileged children access to a good education.*

Autor: Florian Otte, Schwarmstedt
Textquelle: http://mobius.blog.franklintempleton.com/2017/03/16/south-africa-key-issues-and-challenges/ March 16, 2017
© 2018. Franklin Templeton Investments. All rights reserved.

Course: _____   Date: _____   Name: _____

Reading

1 TRUE OR FALSE? *Read the text. Tick the correct box and give the line numbers and the first and last three words of the quote from the text to prove your answers.*

		TRUE	FALSE
1.	Education has become a priority for South African parents. l./ll.: _____		
2.	There are enough school facilities for all school-age children. l./ll.: _____		
3.	In the past, school principals often stole money and used illegal methods to get their positions. l./ll.: _____		
4.	Private schools are restricted to rich people only. l./ll.: _____		
5.	Even poor people are willing to cut back and lower their living standards for the best education of their children. l./ll.: _____		
6.	All schools run by the government are of poor quality. l./ll.: _____		
7.	The quality of education in government schools depends on the location of the school. l./ll.: _____		
8.	In private schools, teacher quality is a problem because of the apartheid years when there was not enough teacher training for blacks. l./ll.: _____		

2 SENTENCE COMPLETION *Read the text and complete the sentences below. Use your own words.*

1. Good education is a prerequisite for _____

2. The three main reasons for poor-quality education in South Africa are _____

_____

3. Trying to provide the best education possible for their children, parents _____

_____

4. In some government schools a good level of education is ensured by _____

_____

5. As it is difficult to hire qualified teachers it is very common to find _____

_____

Course: _____ Date: _____ Name: _____

Reading and writing

Playing the enemy by John Carlin

"Justice Bekebeke was an angry young black man in November 1985, one of millions. Tall and stick-thin, like an African carving[1], he had a courteous manner and a soothing baritone voice that when he spoke
5 carried a wisdom, hard won, beyond his twenty-four years.

Paballelo was where Bekebeke lived, a treeless township five hundred miles north of Mandela's Cape Town prison and five hundred west of Johannesburg,
10 on the edge of the Kalahari Desert, in the back of beyond. A black township in South Africa was always paired with a white town. But while the townships invariably had a lot more people in them, only the white towns appeared on the maps. The townships
15 were the black shadows of the towns. Paballelo was the black shadow of Upington.

Upington was a stark caricature of an apartheid town. An incurious[2] visitor to a big city like Johannesburg might have missed the system's
20 crasser racist edges. But in Upington those edges were sharp and blatant[3] — "Slegs Blankes" ("Whites Only") signs at the public toilets, bars, drinking fountains, cinemas, public swimming pools, parks, bus stops, the railway station. Such nonsense, legally
25 required by the Separate Amenities Act of 1953, sometimes generated dark comedy. Should a black woman carrying her "madam's" white baby travel in the "whites only" or "nonwhites" section of a train? Or would a Japanese visitor who used a "whites only"
30 public toilet be breaking the law? Or what was a bus conductor to do when he ordered a brown-skinned passenger to get off a whites-only bus and the passenger refused, insisting that he was a white man with a deep suntan?
35   […] Paballelo was poorer, dingier, and more cramped than Upington, but less stifling. There you could escape apartheid's pettier constraints. You could eat, shop, or sit wherever you pleased.

[…]The contrast between one place and the other, as always when you crossed over the white world to the
40 black world in South Africa, was staggering, as if you had gone back a century, or stepped straight from suburban Connecticut into Burkina Faso[4]. One was bone-dry, a cramped labyrinth of matchbox houses on a flat expanse of scrub[5], the other was a man-
45 made oasis of weeping willows, golf-green lawns, lovingly tended rose gardens, and large homes whose owners had not been shy about sucking up the resources of the nearby Orange River. Upington would have been almost gracious, had it been less
50 unnatural, had the greenery not smacked of[6] fake adornment[7] amid the obliterating heat and desert drabness all around, had it not been a place where white people routinely called black people by that most hurtful, shaming of names, "kaffir"– South
55 Africa's version of "nigger".

Three childhood memories had a lasting effect on the man Justice Bekebeke would become. The first dated from early in his childhood when he visited Cape Town with his family. Looking out over the
60 Atlantic Ocean, he spotted a speck of land not far offshore. His father, who was barely literate but knew where he stood politically, told him that this was the place where "our leaders" were. The speck was Robben Island. Justice begged his father for a coin to
65 put into a shoreline telescope so he could catch a glimpse of his leaders. He did not succeed, the island being seven miles away, but he saw the outlines of the buildings where the cells were—enough for him to construct a fantasy in his mind that he had actually
70 been to the island. He went back home and recounted the fantasy as fact, impressing his school friends so much that before he knew it he had acquired the Status in Paballelo as a leader himself, as someone from whom his young peers were
75 prepared to take political direction.

(625 words)
From: *Playing the enemy* by John Carlin

---

1 carving artistic design or object carved from wood or stone ● **2 incurious** not interested in knowing or discovering sth ● **3 blatant** obvious, unmistakable ● **4 Burkina Faso** country in western Africa ● **5 scrub** short trees and bushes adapted to a dry climate ● **6 to smack of** to strongly indicate sth unpleasant ● **7 adornment** decorative object, ornament

Autor: Florian Otte, Schwarmstedt
Textquelle: "Playing the Enemy" by John Carlin, Penguin Books 2008, pp. 37-39, ISBN13: 978-0143115724

Course: _____   Date: _____   Name: _____

1 COMPREHENSION

Outline the circumstances Justice Bekebeke found himself in as a child. Consider the time, place and his personal experiences.

2 ANALYSIS

Analyse the language and stylistic devices the author uses to compare the settlements Paballelo and Upington.

3 EVALUATION

a) *Discuss whether a poor and underprivileged childhood can help prepare somebody for a political career. Refer to the excerpt and to your own knowledge.*

OR

b) *Imagine you are Justice Bekebeke speaking to the city council of Upington before the end of apartheid. In your speech you demand that townships like Paballelo 'appear on the maps' and are not forgotten any longer.*

Reading

1 SENTENCE COMPLETION

Read the text and then complete the following sentences.

1. Considering his age, Bekebeke was an exceptional young man because _____

    _____ and _____

2. The author calls Paballelo the "black shadow" of Upington because _____

    _____

3. The author calls Upington a "caricature" of an apartheid town because _____

    _____

4. The author uses humour to reveal _____

5. Given the choice to live in one of the settlements, the author would have preferred _____

    because _____

6. The author refers to suburban Connecticut and Burkina Faso to _____

    _____

7. The author does not appreciate the beautiful gardens of Upington because *(3 items)* _____

    _____

    _____

8. Bekebeke's father explained to his son that their leaders _____

9. Bekebeke was disappointed because _____

10. Bekebeke's fellow students were naïve because _____

    _____

Course: _____   Date: _____   Name: _____

Listening

◎ **Electricity crisis in South Africa**

1   MULTIPLE CHOICE

Listen to a report about the electricity crisis in South Africa. You will hear the report twice.
Before listening, you will have three minutes to read through the tasks. After listening for the first time, you will
have two minutes to fill in your answers. After listening for the second time, you will have four minutes to
complete the tasks.
Tick the correct answer(s). There can be more than one correct answer.

1. The Soweto Electricity Crisis Committee
    ☐ a) started in January 2010.
    ☐ b) has a good relationship to the electricity
       provider.
    ☐ c) argues that township people have a right
       to free electricity.
    ☐ d) started before apartheid.

2. Zodwa Madiba has not paid any electricity
    bills for
    ☐ a) a year.
    ☐ b) three years.
    ☐ c) ten years.
    ☐ d) more than 15 years.

3. According to Zodwa Madiba, they have stolen
    electricity for
    ☐ a) a few poor people.
    ☐ b) hundreds of people.
    ☐ c) thousands of people.
    ☐ d) half a million people.

4. The people of Soweto owe the electricity company
    Eskom approximately
    ☐ a) $3 million.
    ☐ b) $50 million.
    ☐ c) $100 million.
    ☐ d) $300 million.

5. Escom, the electricity company,
    ☐ a) is making a lot of profit.
    ☐ b) is taking their pre-payment meters away
       from Soweto.
    ☐ c) has limited the amount of electricity for the
       whole population.
    ☐ d) argues that not paying for electricity makes
       it more difficult to help poor people.

6. According to Zodwa Madiba,
    ☐ a) electricity should be cheaper for companies.
    ☐ b) riots will continue unless a solution is
       found.
    ☐ c) wealthy people consume too much electricity.
    ☐ d) electricity should be free for everyone.

7. In the riot described in the report,
    ☐ a) two men were injured.
    ☐ b) cash machines were destroyed.
    ☐ c) people didn't use any weapons.
    ☐ d) windows of a hotel were smashed.

8. The people who were involved in the riot
    ☐ a) have never had electricity.
    ☐ b) all have a job.
    ☐ c) live in a run-down area of Cape Town.
    ☐ d) hadn't had electricity for a couple of days.

Autor: Florian Otte, Schwarmstedt

Klett

Course: _____ Date: _____ Name: _____

Listening

⊙ **Truth And Reconciliation in South Africa**

SHORT ANSWERS
Listen to the BBC host Max Pearson and Milton Nkosi talking about the introduction of the Truth and Reconciliation Commission (TRC) after the end of apartheid. Answer the questions in keywords – you do not have to write complete sentences. The first exercise is given as an example.

0. How long was Nelson Mandela imprisoned?

 For 27 years _____

1. What did Mandela mean by "Let bygones be bygones"?

 _____

2. Why did Nelson Mandela think that the Truth and Reconciliation Commission (TRC) had been necessary for South African society?

 _____

3. Why were a lot of people angry about the TRC?

 _____

4. According to Milton Nkosi, why do a lot of the perpetrators live a better lifestyle than people in the black townships *(Give three items.)*?

 _____

 _____

 _____

5. How did Nelson Mandela succeed in establishing the TRC?

 _____

6. How successful has the truth and reconciliation process been?

 _____

7. How does Milton Nkosi describe the government?

 _____

8. What is one of the new political party's aims?

 _____

9. When did the problem with injustice start according to Milton Nkosi?

 _____

10. After listening: why is Milton Nkosi a reliable person for information about the years before and after apartheid?

 _____

Klett

Course: _____   Date: _____   Name: _____

Mediation

Together with your partner school in Cape Town, you are doing a project on the post-apartheid era in South Africa.
You have been asked to write a report about slum tourism in South Africa for the next video conference.
Write your report with the information from the article below.

Im Wohnzimmer der Armen

Weltweit boomt der Slum-Tourismus: Urlauber aus Europa besuchen zu Tausenden Armenviertel in Rio de Janeiro, Kapstadt oder Johannesburg. Manche halten das für eine neue Form der Entwicklungshilfe
5 – andere für Armutspornografie.
Beim Eintritt in die Wellblechhütte fallen die Touristen aus ihrer Luxuswolke. Es gibt nur ein kleines Fensterchen, die Luft riecht leicht faulig. Kenny Tokwe deutet auf eine Pfütze neben dem Bett.
10 "Gestern hat es geregnet", sagt er. "Die ganze Wohnung wird dann feucht." Die Bewohner hocken versunken in einem Sessel, die Besucher schweigen. Wie fast immer: "Die Leute sind meistens überfordert und wissen nicht, was sie sagen sollen", erklärt
15 Tokwe später.[…]
Manche halten den Slum-Tourismus für eine Form der Entwicklungshilfe, ein Mittel zur Armutsbekämpfung – andere für Pornografie der Armut.
20 "Die Vergleiche mit einer Menschensafari sind weit verbreitet", sagt Malte Steinbrink von der Universität Osnabrück, einer der führenden Slum-Tourismus-Forscher weltweit. "Meine Beobachtungen und Gespräche geben aber kaum Hinweise darauf, dass
25 die Touristen von den Bewohnern als Voyeure wahrgenommen werden – den meisten ist deren Anwesenheit ziemlich egal." Manche entwickelten auch Stolz auf ihr Viertel, sagt Steinbrink. "Anders ist es, wenn in die Privatsphäre eingedrungen wird oder
30 beim hemmungslosen Fotografieren." […]
Tokwe will Touristen das Leben der anderen zeigen. Nicht verklärt, aber auch nicht dramatisiert. Mit seiner Familie lebt er selbst in der Township, die Einnahmen fließen nicht in die Kasse eines großen Veranstalters.
35 Knapp sechs Euro zahlen Besucher für eine zweistündige Tour. Die Hälfte bekommt Tokwe

als Lohn, ein Euro geht an die Familien, deren Hütten besichtigt werden. Damit werde niemand aus der Armut geholt, räumt Tokwe ein. Der Betrag sei eher eine Aufwandsentschädigung. Mit dem Rest des 40 Geldes werden Projekte in Imizamo Yethu finanziert, ein Computerkurs für Kinder zum Beispiel oder ein Gemüsegarten hinter der Schule.
"Der Aspekt der Hilfe wird von Touranbietern und Touristen häufig als Rechtfertigung angeführt, um 45 ethischen Zweifeln zu begegnen", sagt Slumtourismusforscher Steinbrink. "Aber wer helfen möchte, braucht wirklich keine Slum-Besichtigung zu machen." Armutstourismus als probates Mittel zur Armutsreduzierung – das erscheint Steinbrink 50 unbegründet. Meist würden nur Einzelne profitieren, außerdem kämen die meisten Anbieter von außerhalb, weil es wie in Rio de Janeiro Sprachbarrieren gibt oder Bewohner selbst nicht über Kapital für eine eigene Firma verfügen. 55
Steinbrink sieht eine weitere Gefahr dieser Führungen: Vorher würden die meisten Touristen Dreck, Elend und Gewalt mit den Slums verbinden. "Nach einer Tour sind viele aber richtig beseelt und berichten von intensiven, positiven Erlebnissen." Die 60 Art, wie Armenviertel oft gezeigt würden, könne zu einer "Entpolitisierung" führen: Slums würden nicht mehr als Probleme wahrgenommen, nicht als Orte sozialer und wirtschaftlicher Ungleichheiten, sondern als Ausdruck einer kulturellen Eigenart. 65
Dennoch muss nicht jede Tour schlecht sein. Experten empfehlen Interessierten, sich vor Ort einen kleineren Veranstalter zu suchen. Einheimische Guides sollten die Touren begleiten. Eine kleine Gruppengröße hat den Vorteil, dass der Kontakt zu 70 den Menschen direkter ist. […]

(467 words)
Benjamin Dürr, *Spiegel*, 2013

Course: _____ Date: _____ Name: _____

Writing

How often do you experience racism in your life (all/most of the time)?

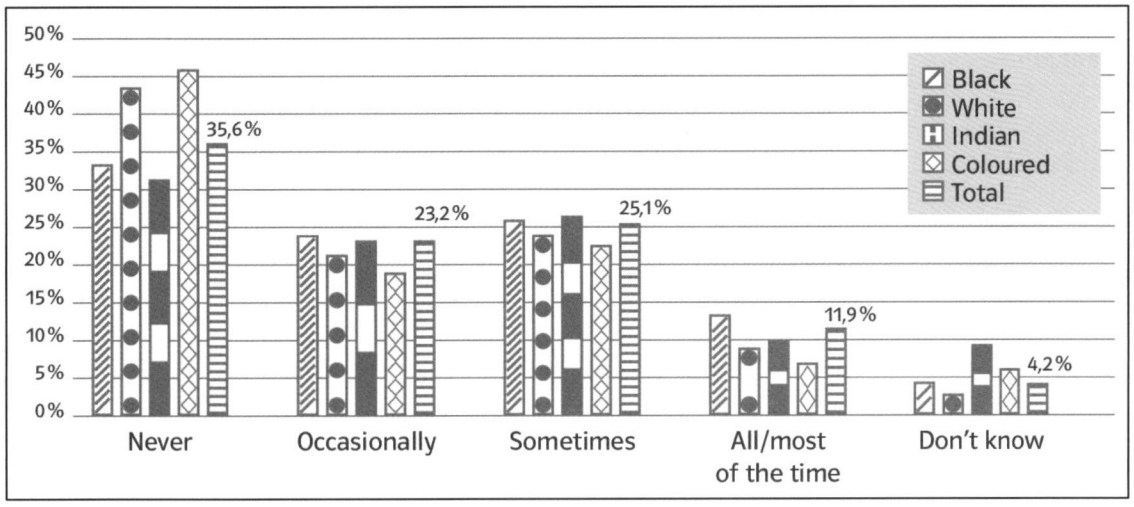

1   *Analyse the statistics.*

2   *Choose one of the tasks:*

a) *The statement below is taken from a comment about violence against Asian and African immigrants in South Africa. The writer argues that the "miracle" transition from apartheid to democracy has not improved the situation for black South Africans.*

> "South Africa isn't anti-immigrant, it's anti-black, and this violence is evidence that the "miracle" has failed the very people it should have uplifted – poor black South Africans."

Comment on this statement. In your answer refer to the table above and to what you have learned in class.

OR

b) *Comment on the statement below. In your answer consider what you learned in class.*

> "In South Africa there is a horrible lack of imagination about the future. There are grand plans to build whole new satellite cities outside Cape Town, but they're following the same model of putting the poorest people furthest away. It seems like we're just repeating all the mistakes of the past."

Autor: Florian Otte, Schwarmstedt
Textquellen: 1. © Institute for Justice and Reconciliation, 2015 Jan Hofmeyr and Rajen Govender, NATIONAL RECONCILIATION, RACE RELATIONS, AND SOCIAL INCLUSION, 2015; 2. Copyright Guardian News & Media Ltd 2017; 3. Copyright Guardian News & Media Ltd 2014

Bewertungsraster zu *Reading and Writing*

INHALT (40%)		Erreichte Punkte	Mögliche Punkte
1) Comprehension		Erreichte Punkte	Mögliche Punkte
Fragestellung komplett nahezu komplett im Wesentlichen teilweise kaum bis nicht erfüllt. ⟵————————————————————————⟶ _____ _____ _____ _____ _____ _____ _____			
2) Analysis		Erreichte Punkte	Mögliche Punkte
Textaussage voll nahezu voll im Wesentlichen teilweise kaum bis nicht erfasst. ⟵————————————————————————⟶ _____ _____ _____ _____ _____ _____ _____			
3) Evaluation		Erreichte Punkte	Mögliche Punkte
Aufgabenstellung voll nahezu voll im Wesentlichen teilweise kaum bis nicht erfasst. ⟵————————————————————————⟶ _____ _____ _____ _____ _____ _____ _____			
Gesamtpunktzahl INHALT:			

SPRACHE (60%)	Erreichte Punkte	Mögliche Punkte
1) Kommunikative Textgestaltung		

Aufgabenbezug

voll　　　　　nahezu voll　　　　im Wesentlichen　　　teilweise　　　kaum bis nicht erfüllt.

←——————————————————————————————→

_____

_____

Textaufbau und Darstellung

durchgehend　　　bis auf Details　　　im Wesentlichen　　　teilweise　　　kaum bis nicht überzeugend/stringent.

←——————————————————————————————→

_____

_____

2) Ausdrucksvermögen/Verfügbarkeit sprachlicher Mittel	Erreichte Punkte	Mögliche Punkte

Eigenständige und sichere Formulierung

voll　　　　　nahezu voll　　　　im Wesentlichen　　　teilweise　　　kaum bis nicht gegeben.

←——————————————————————————————→

_____

_____

3) Sprachrichtigkeit	Erreichte Punkte	Mögliche Punkte

Wortschatz:

versiert/　　　versiert/　　　begrenzt/　　　einfach/　　　einfach/
sicher　　　　nahezu sicher　　klar　　　　meist verständlich　　viele Fehler

←——————————————————————————————→

_____

_____

Grammatik:

versiert/　　　versiert/　　　begrenzt/　　　einfach/　　　einfach/
sicher　　　　nahezu sicher　　klar　　　　meist verständlich　　viele Fehler

_____

_____

Orthografie:

nahezu　　　meist　　　einige　　　einige/gravierende　　viele/gravierende
fehlerfrei　　fehlerfrei　　Fehler　　　Fehler　　　　Fehler

_____

Gesamtpunktzahl SPRACHE:		
Gesamtpunktzahl INHALT und SPRACHE:		

Klett

Bewertungsraster zu Sprachmittlung

Anforderungen:		Erreichte Punkte	Mögliche Punkte
INHALT (40%)			
Sinngemäße Zusammenfassung der wesentlichen Inhalte im Sinne der Aufgabenstellung	Situations- und Adressatenbezug		
	Konzentration auf wesentliche/geforderte Inhalte		
	Ggf. Ergänzung zusätzlicher Informationen zu der Herkunftskultur zur Sicherung des Verständnisses		
	Summe INHALT:		
SPRACHE (60%)			
Kommunikative Textgestaltung	Aufgabenbezug/Textformat		
	Textaufbau		
Ausdrucksvermögen/ Verfügbarkeit sprachlicher Mittel	Eigenständige und sichere Formulierung		
Sprachrichtigkeit	Wortschatz		
	Grammatik		
	Orthografie		
	Summe SPRACHE:		
	Gesamtpunktzahl Sprachmittlung:		
	GESAMT		